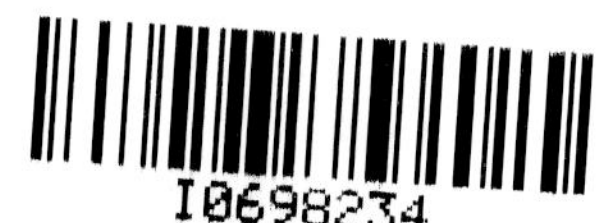

THIS BOOK BELONGS TO

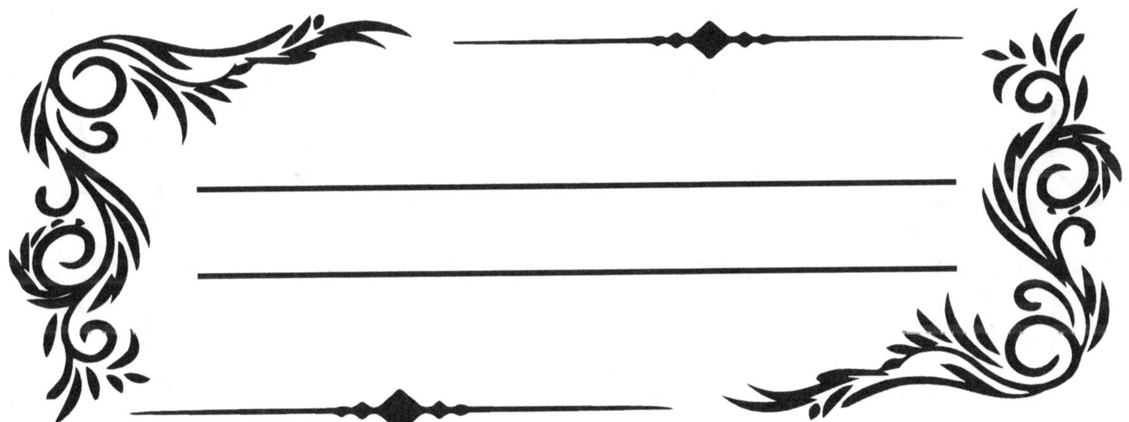

COLOR TEST PAGES

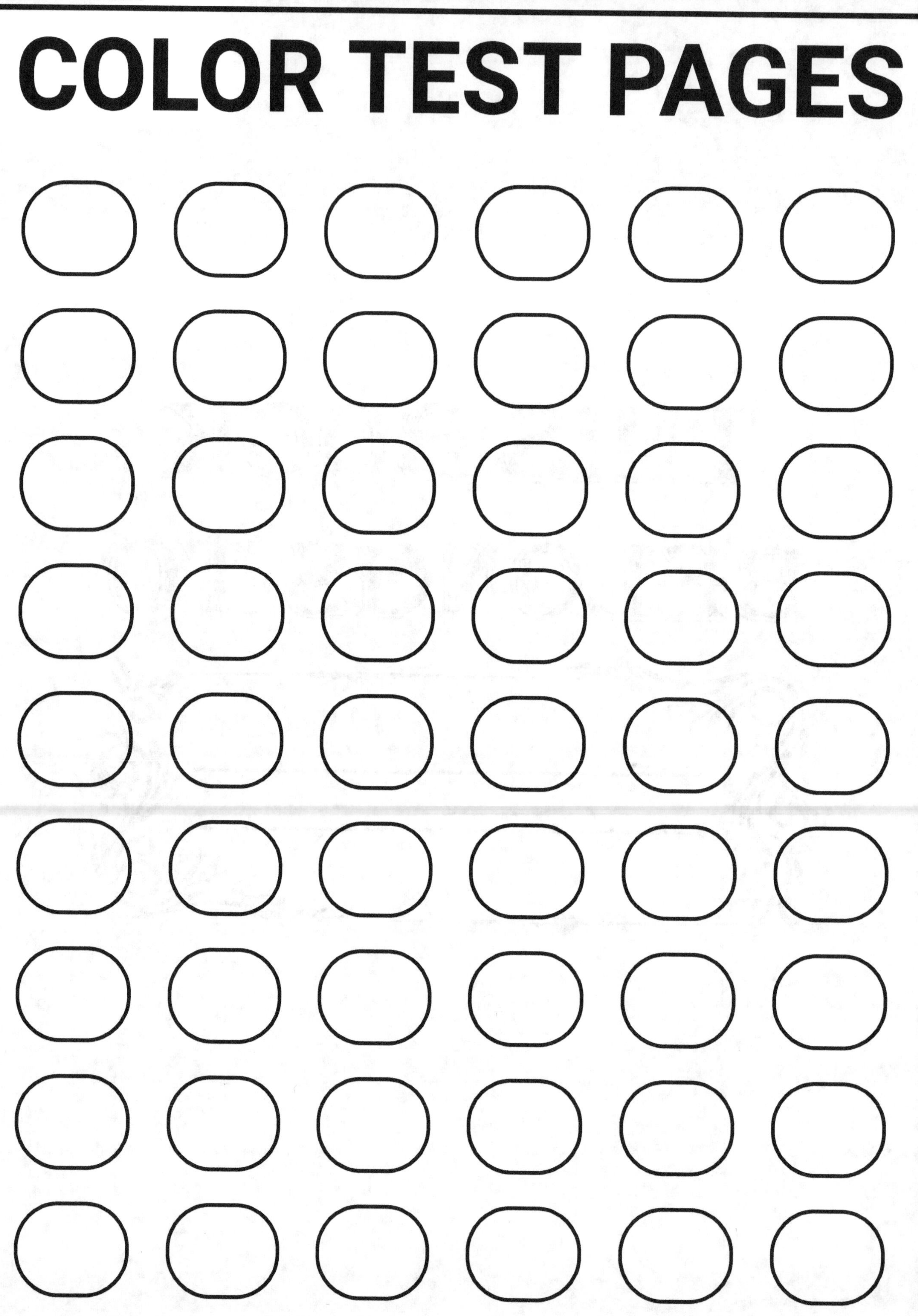

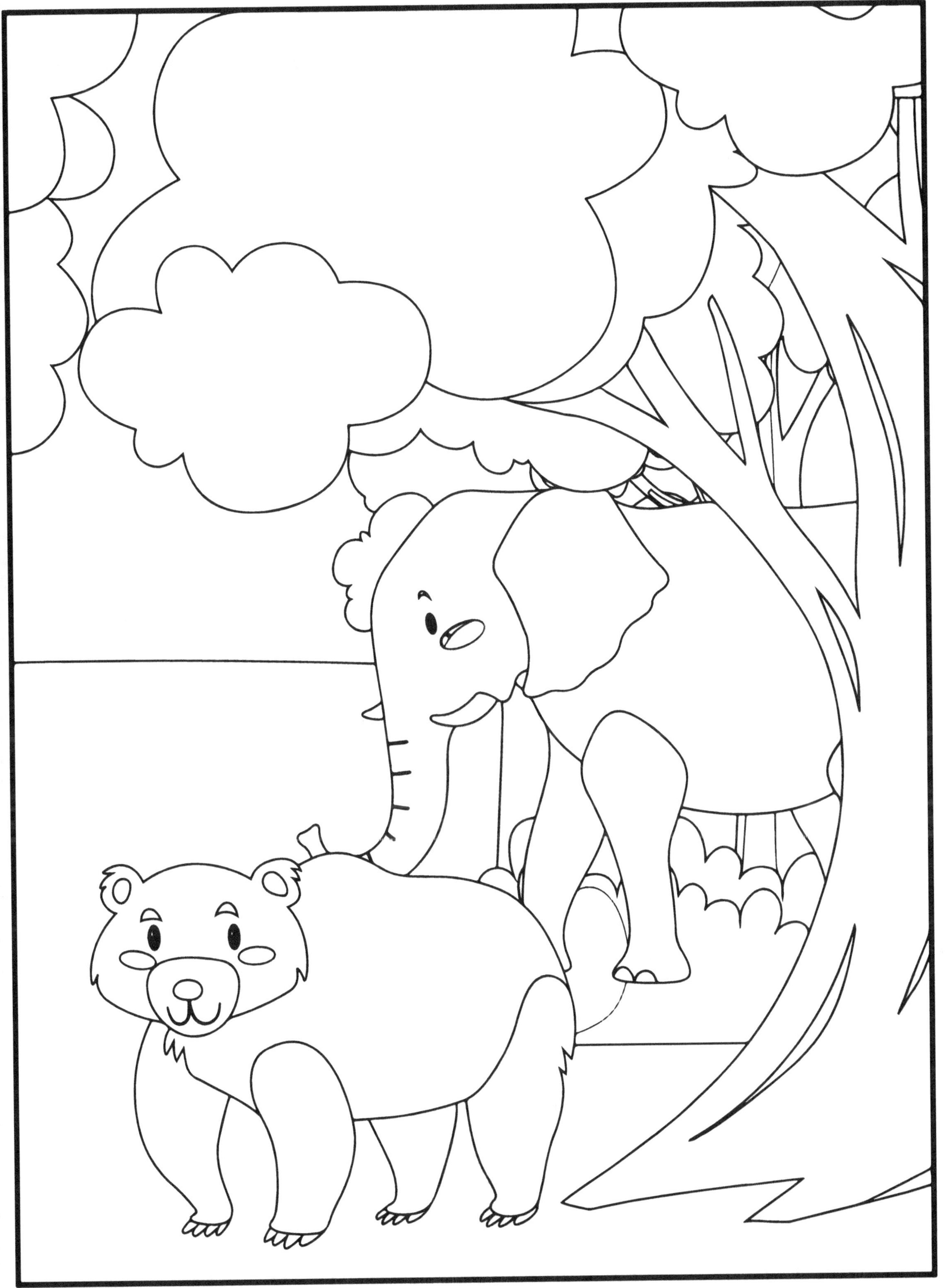

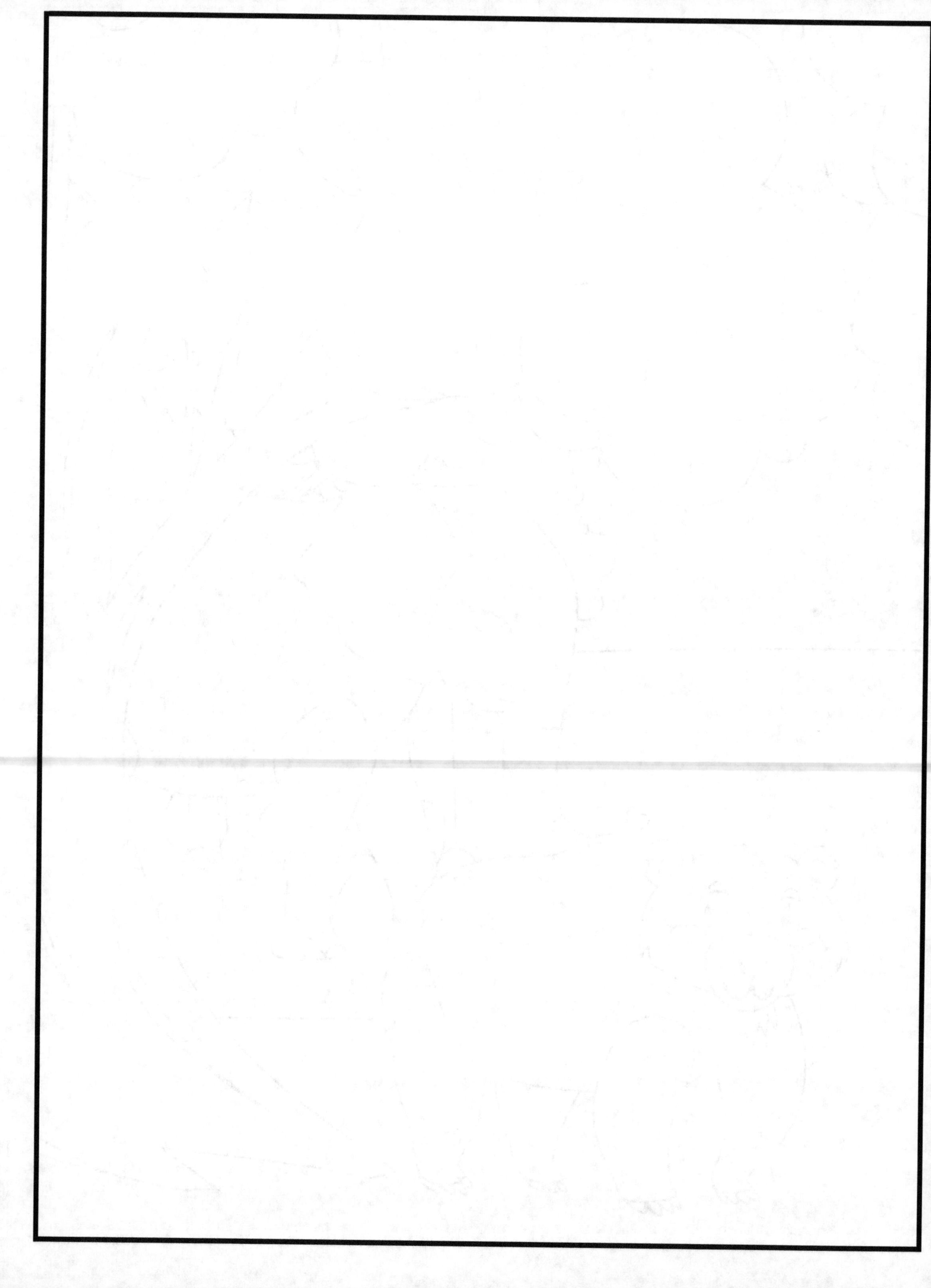

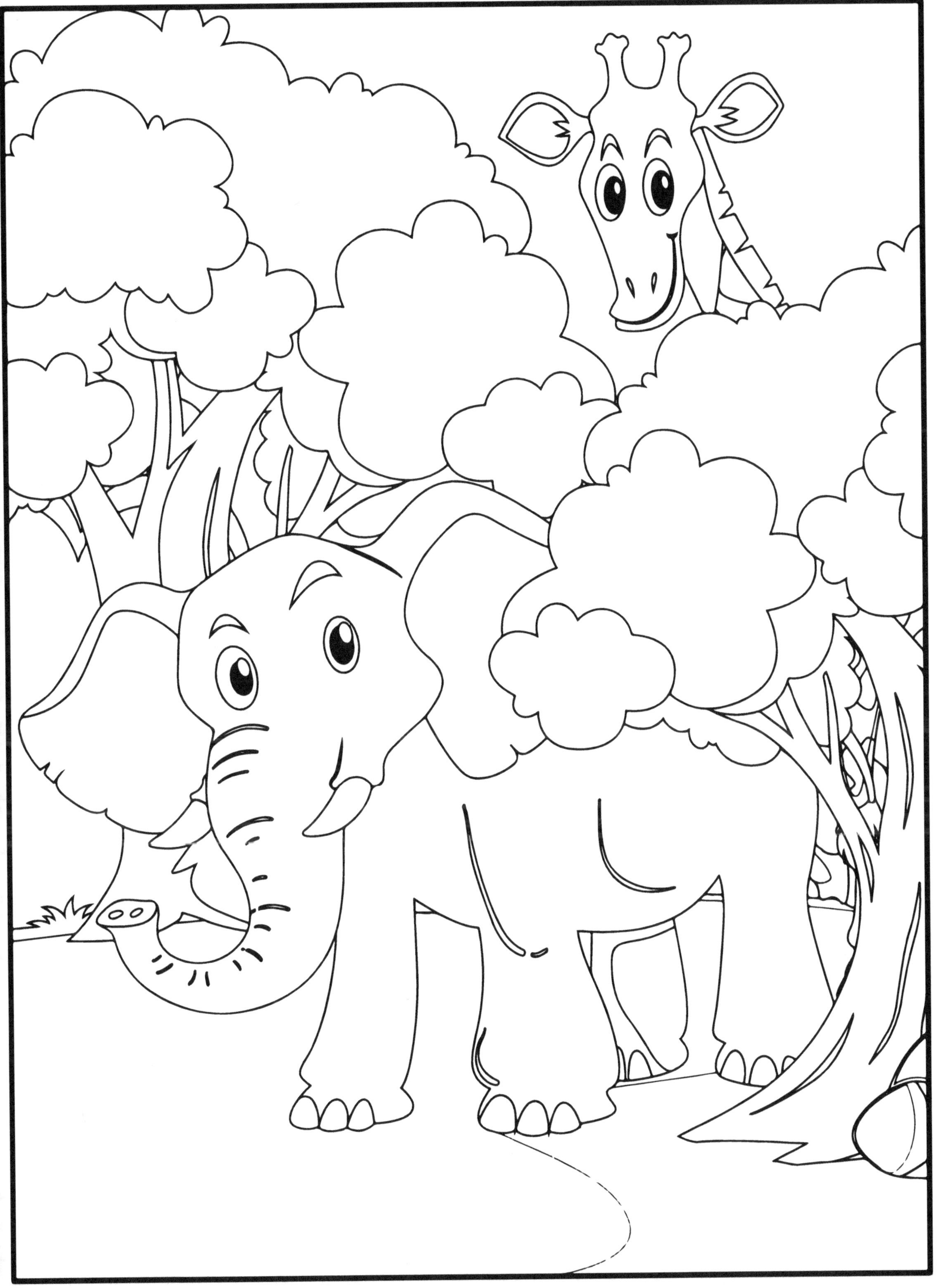

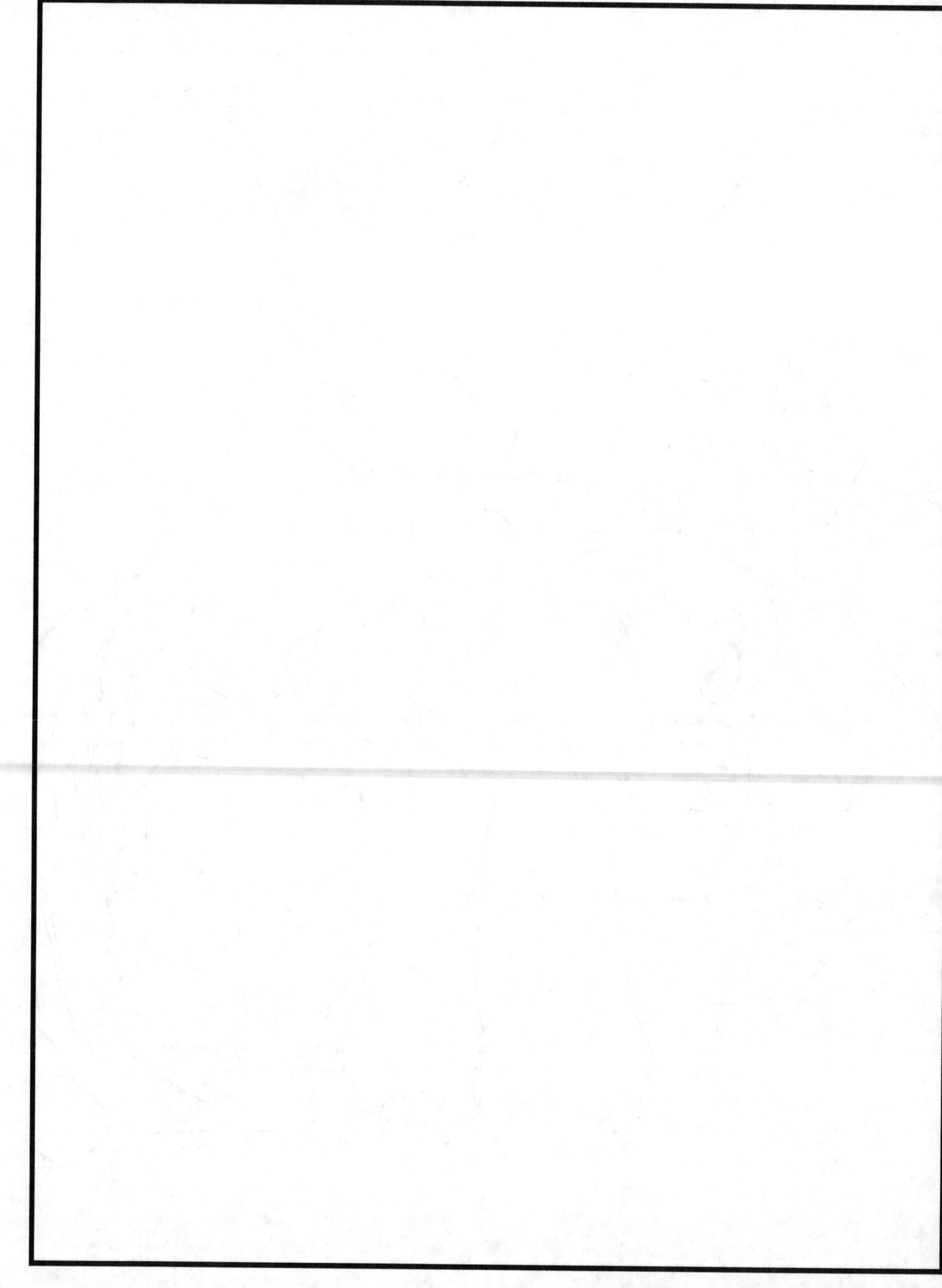

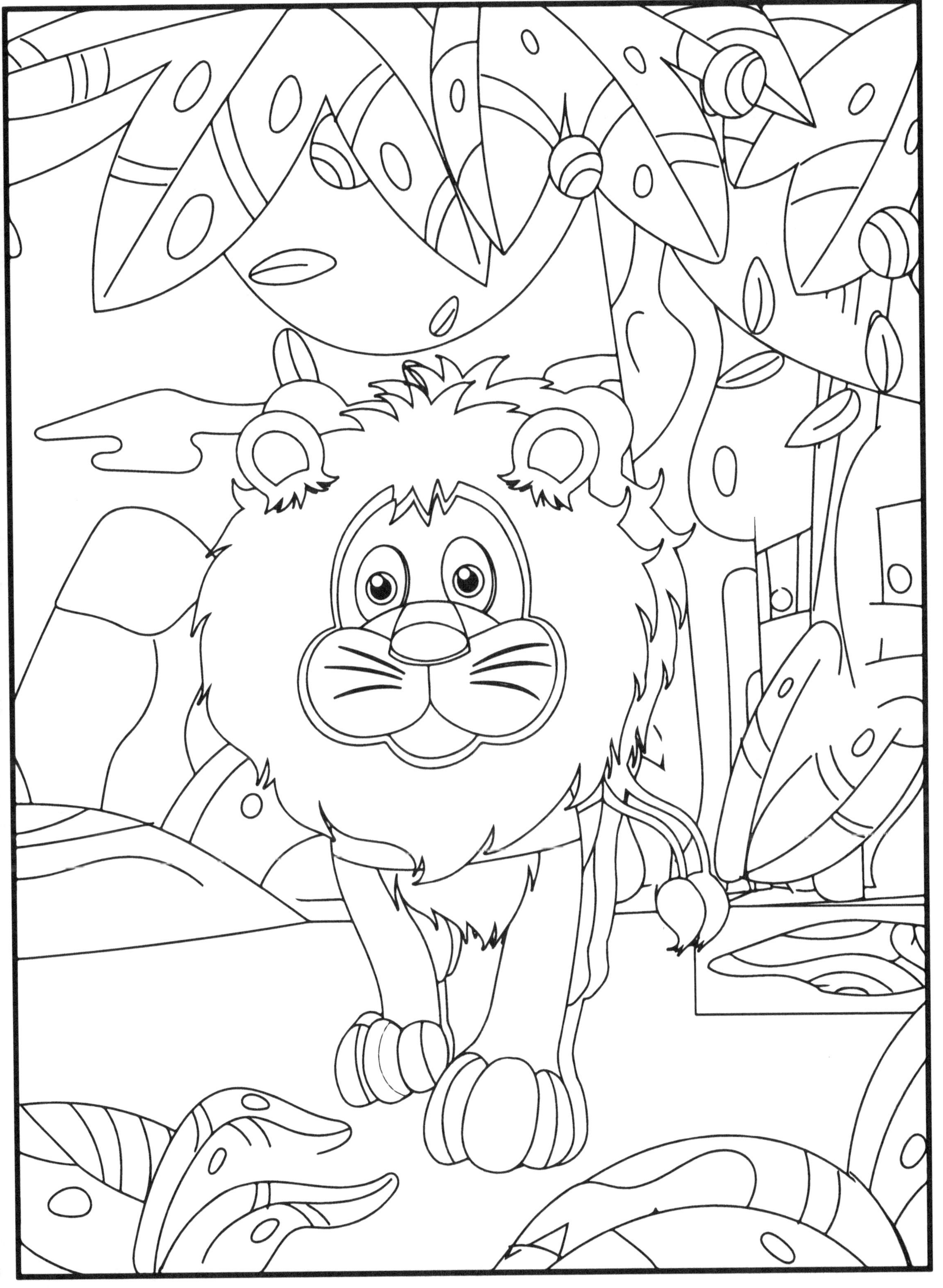

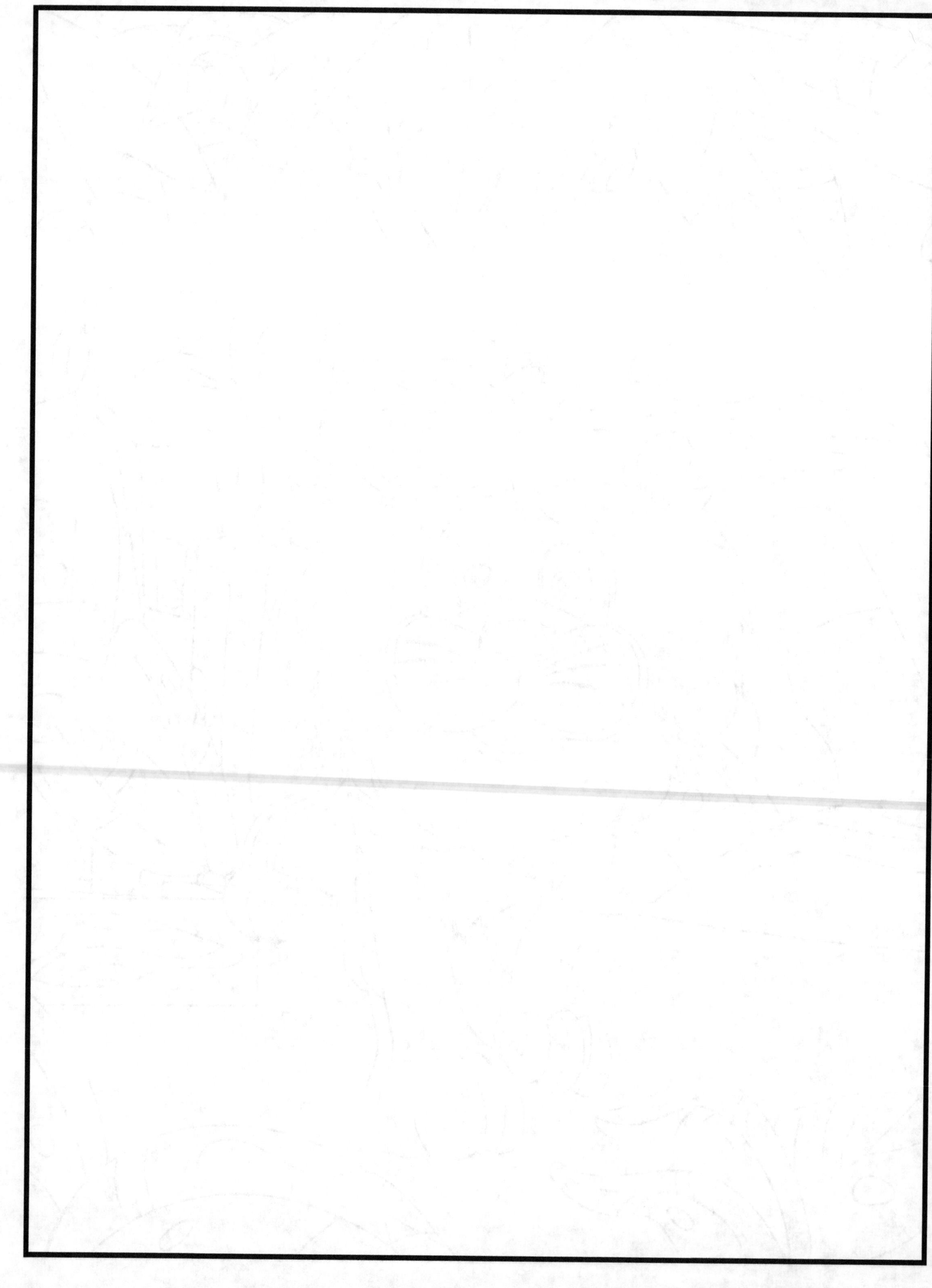

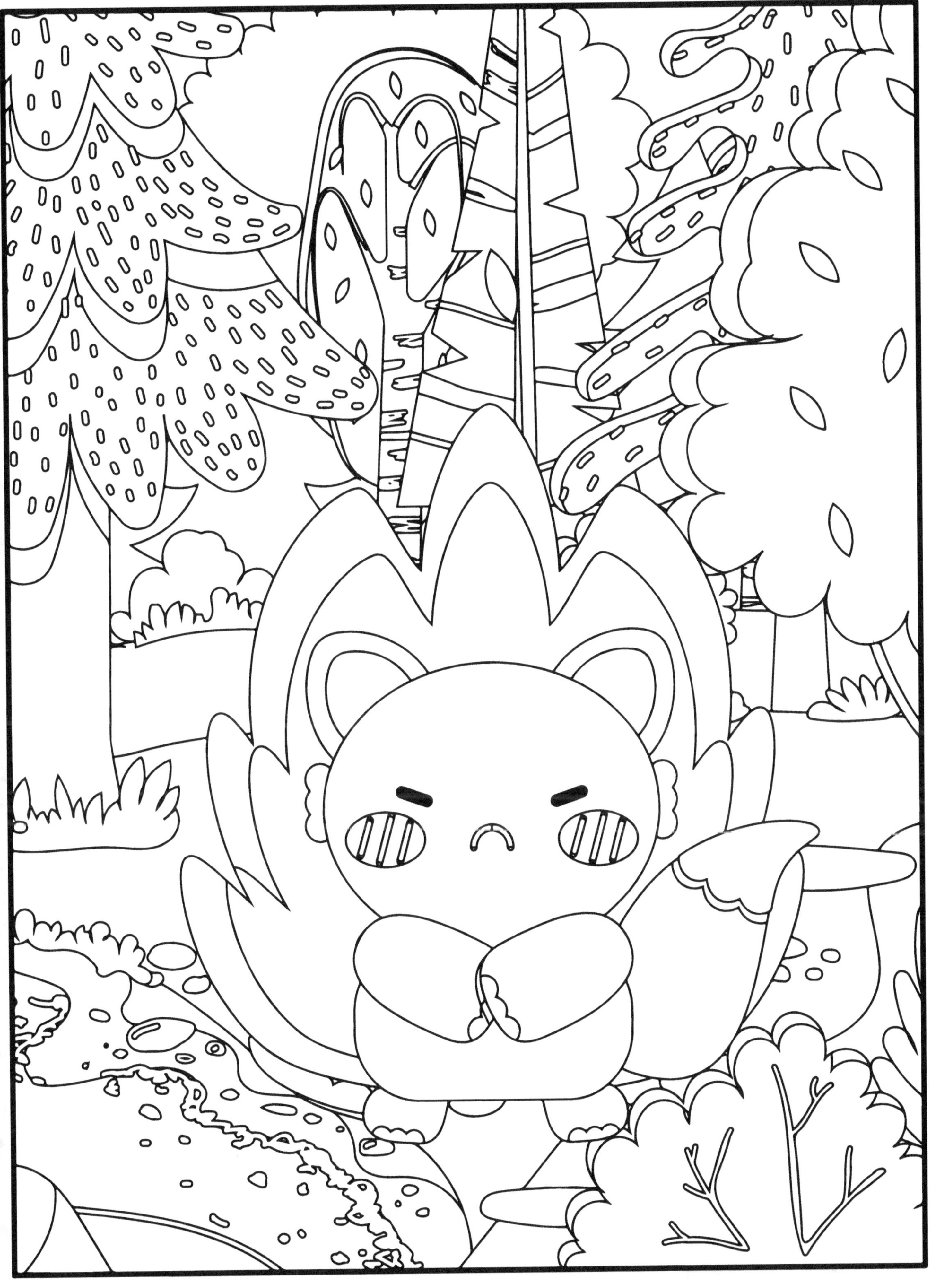

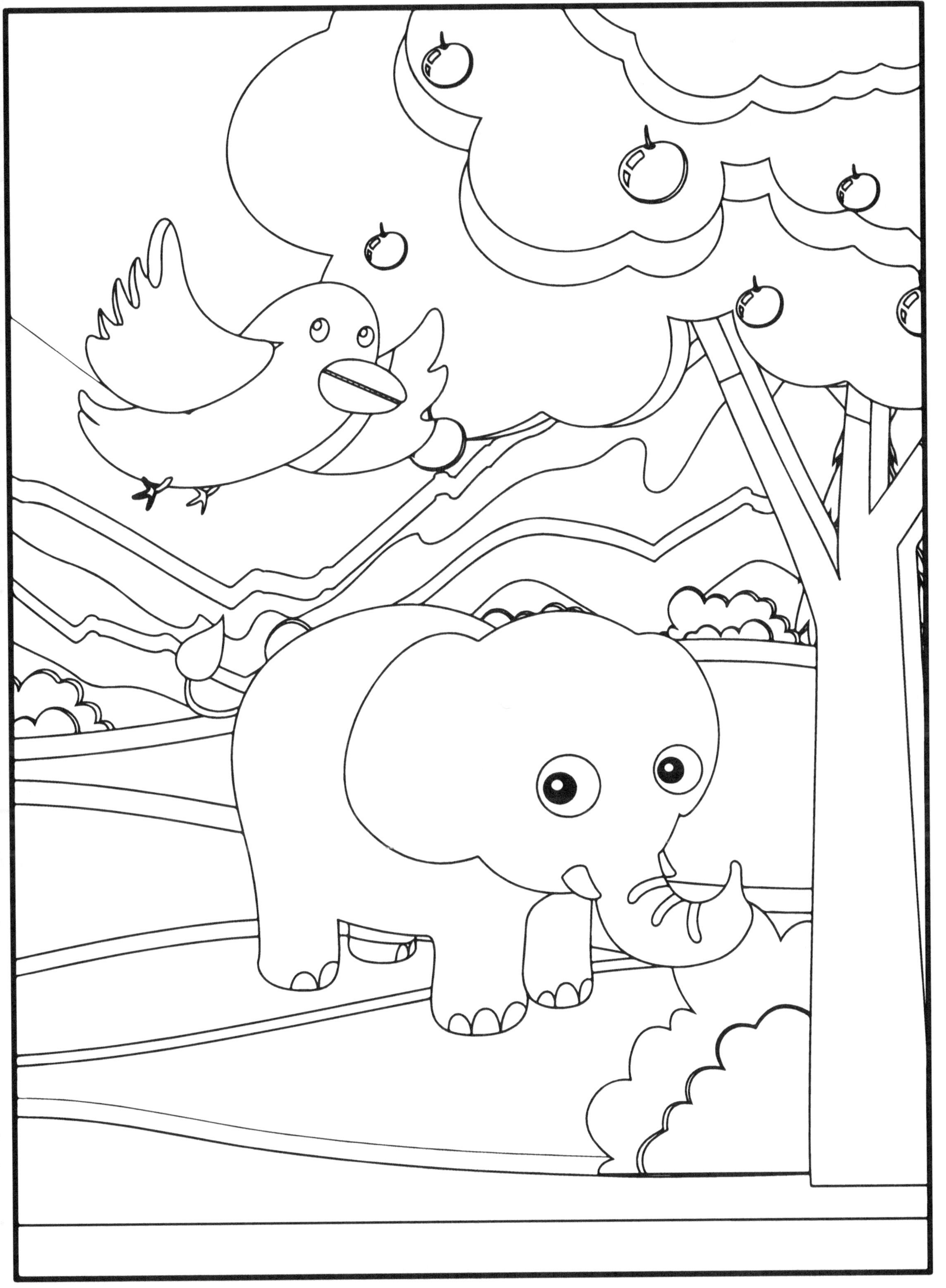

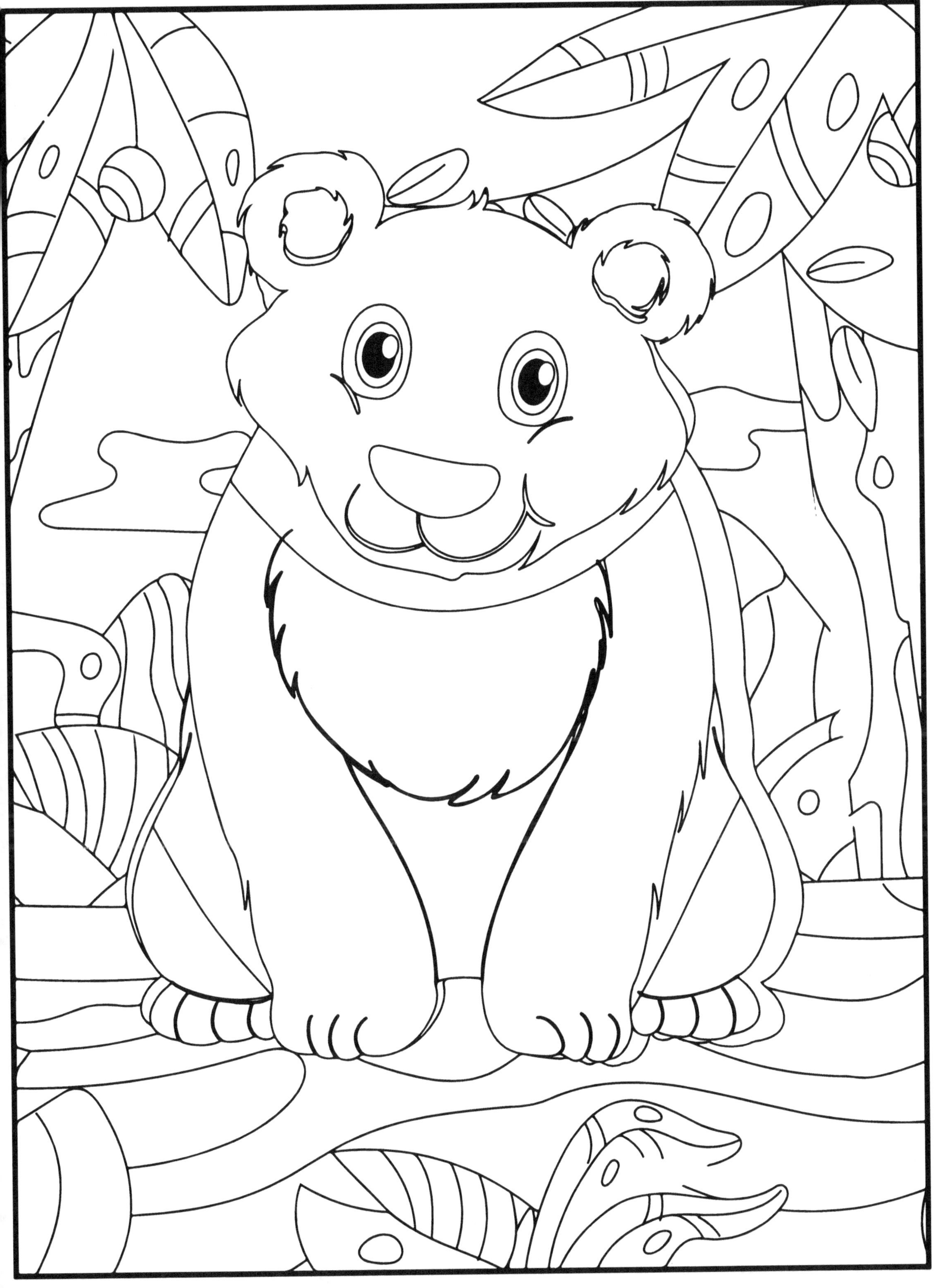

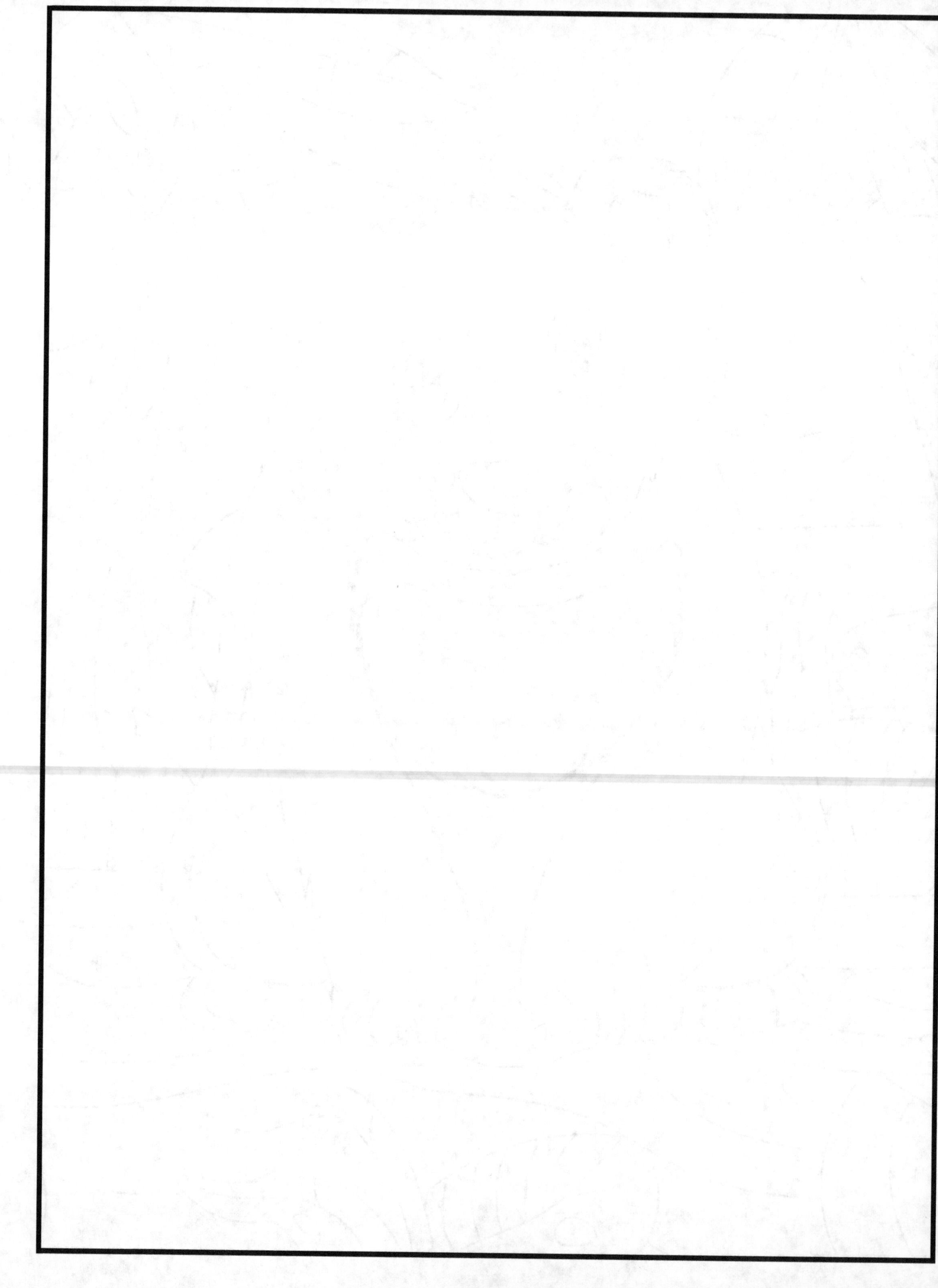

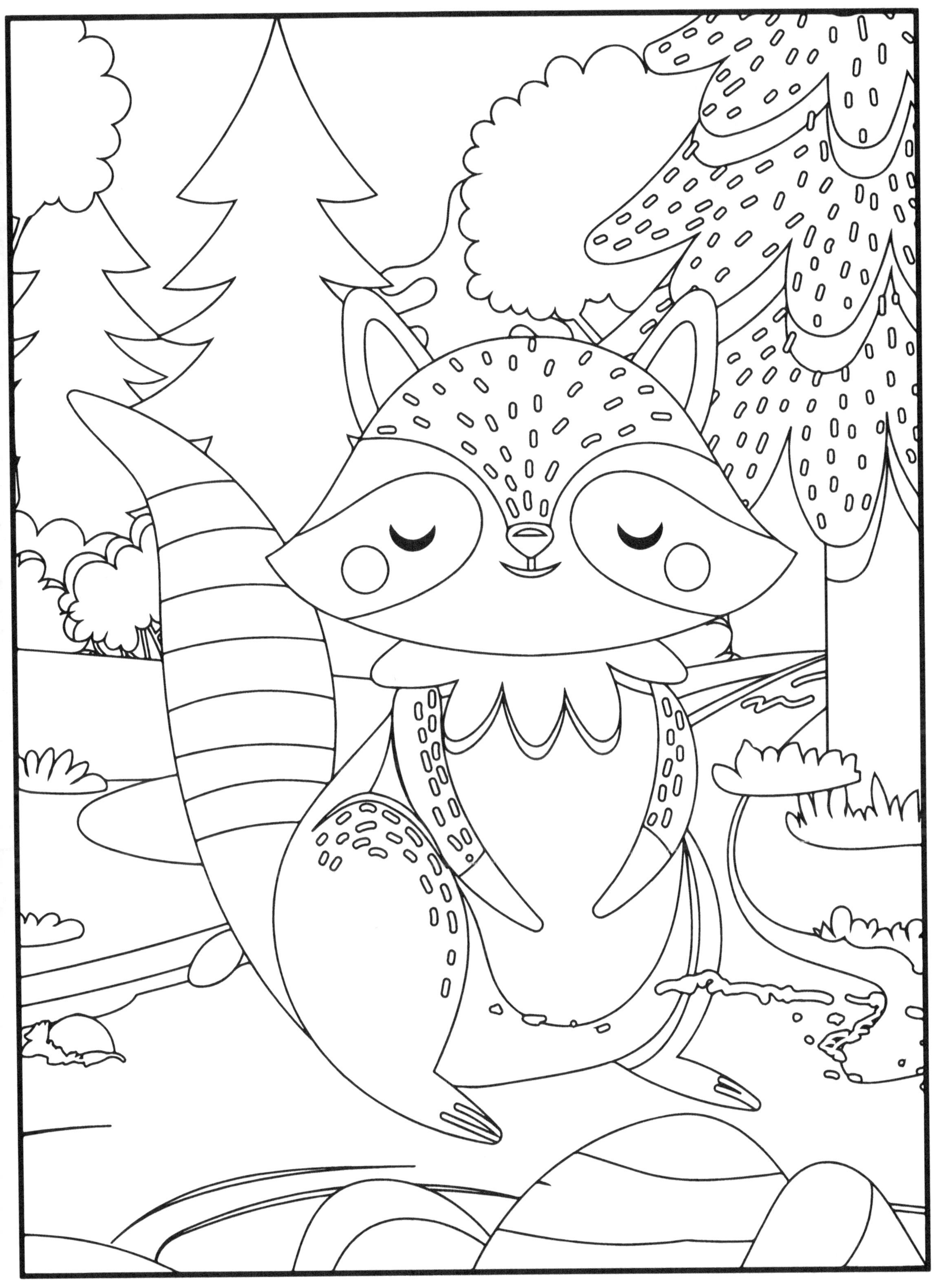

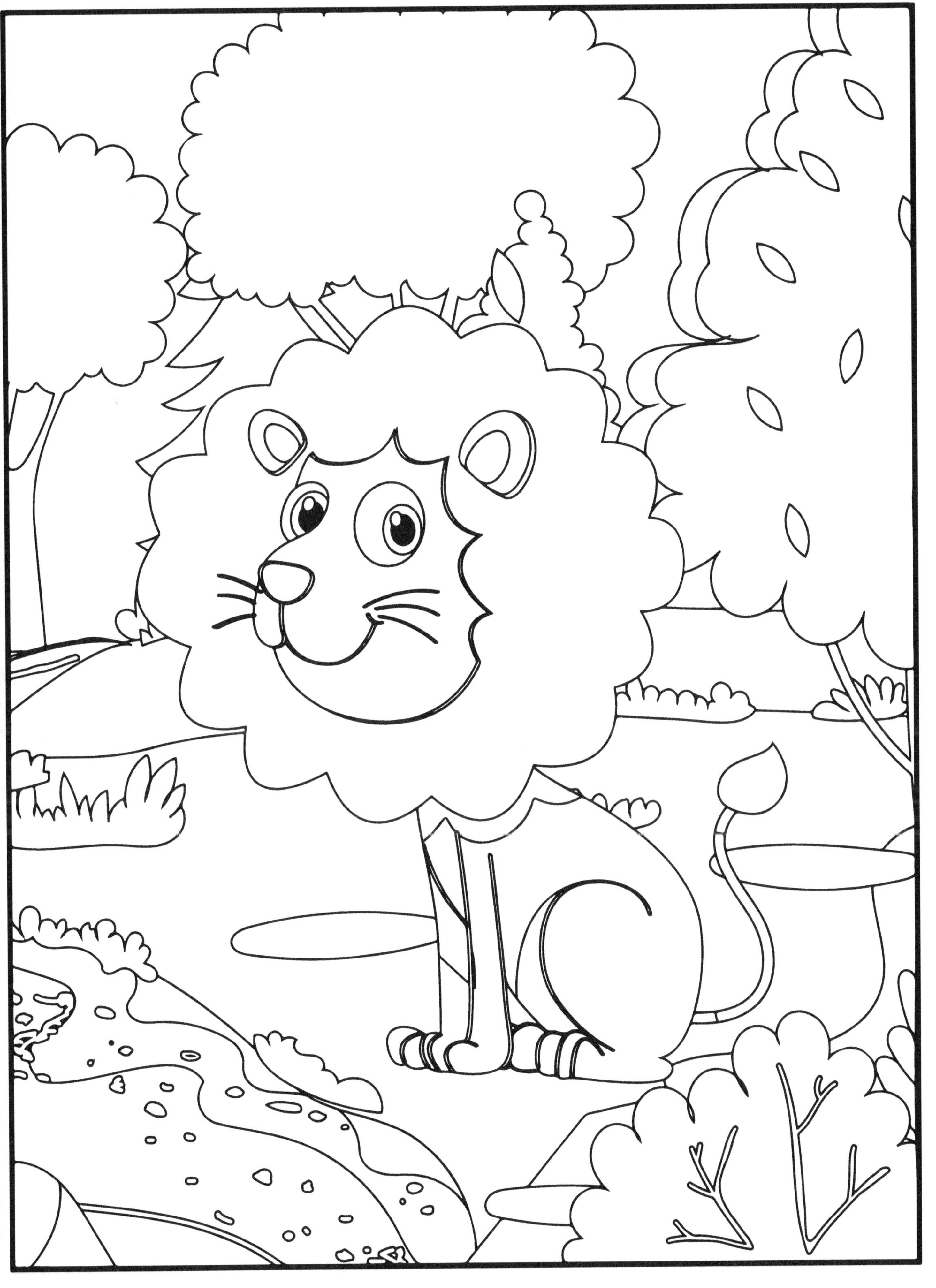

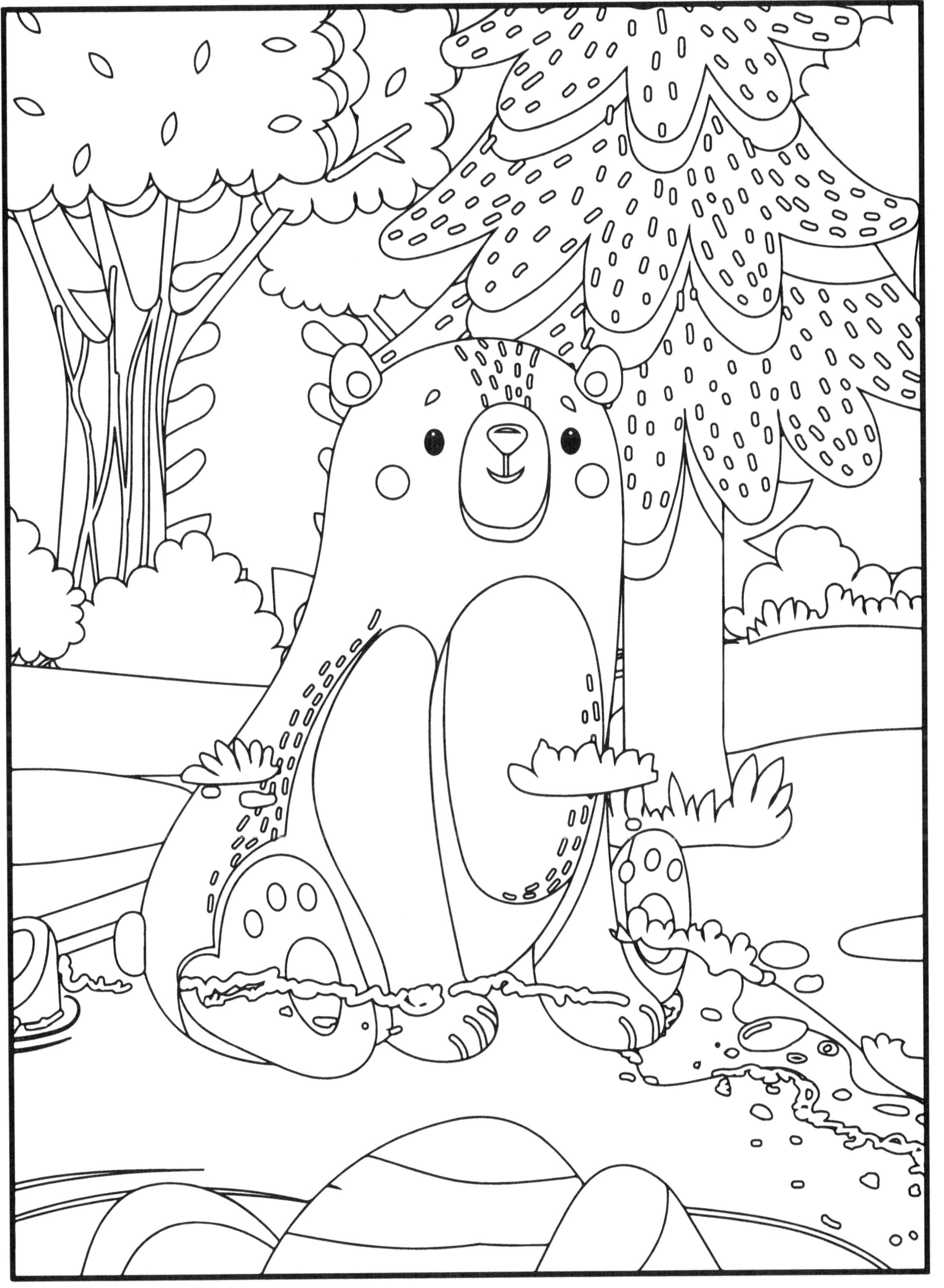

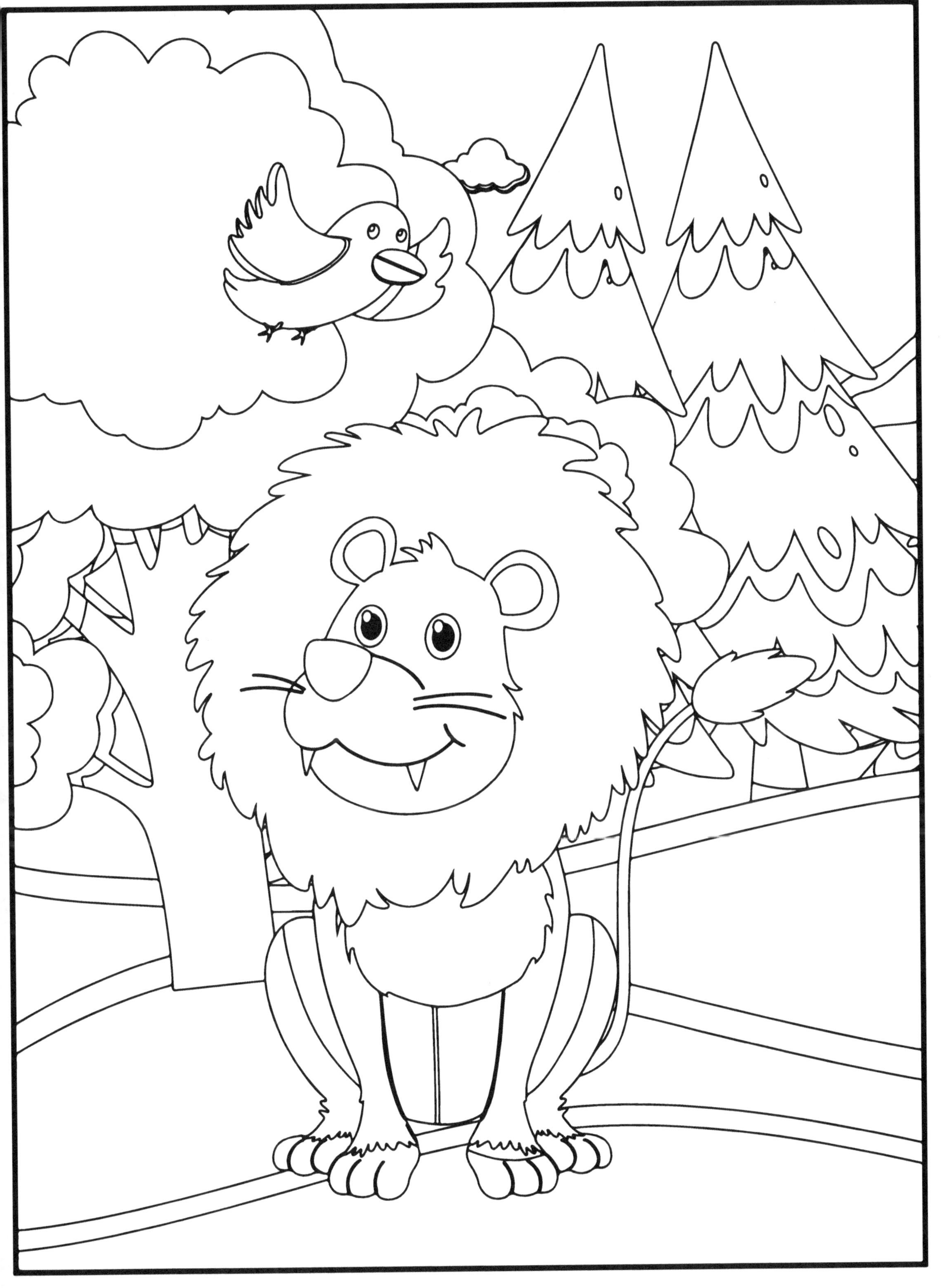

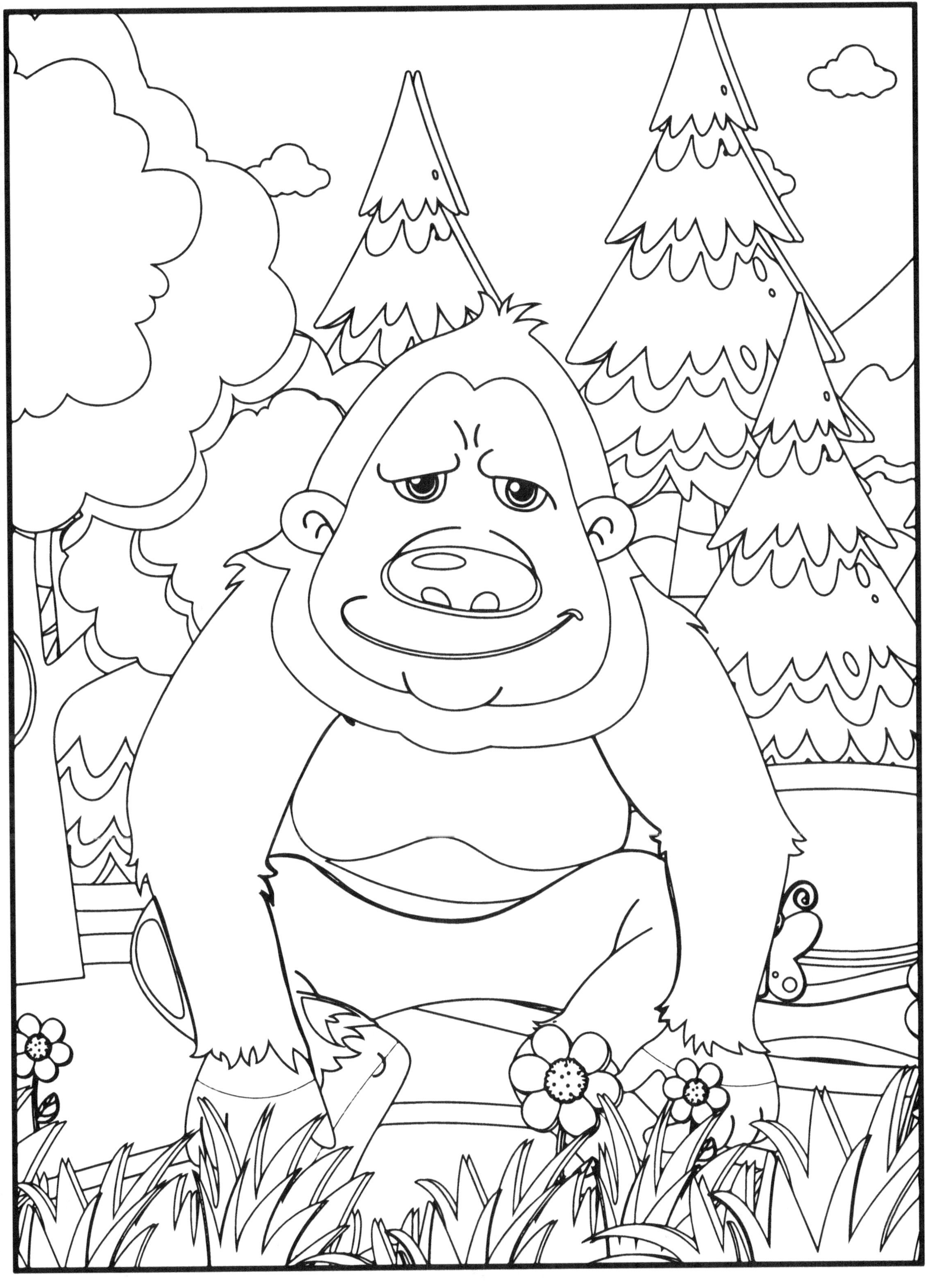

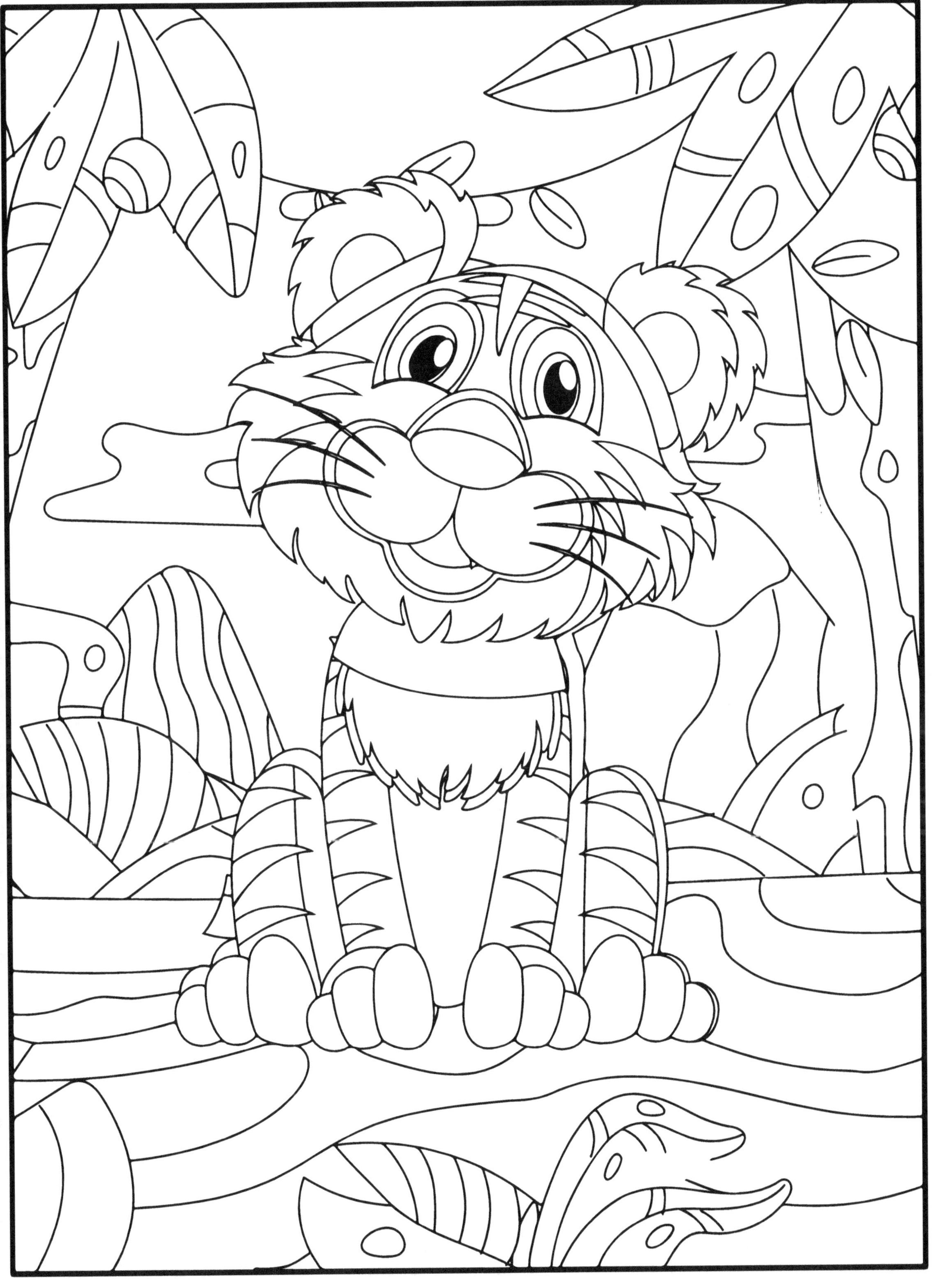

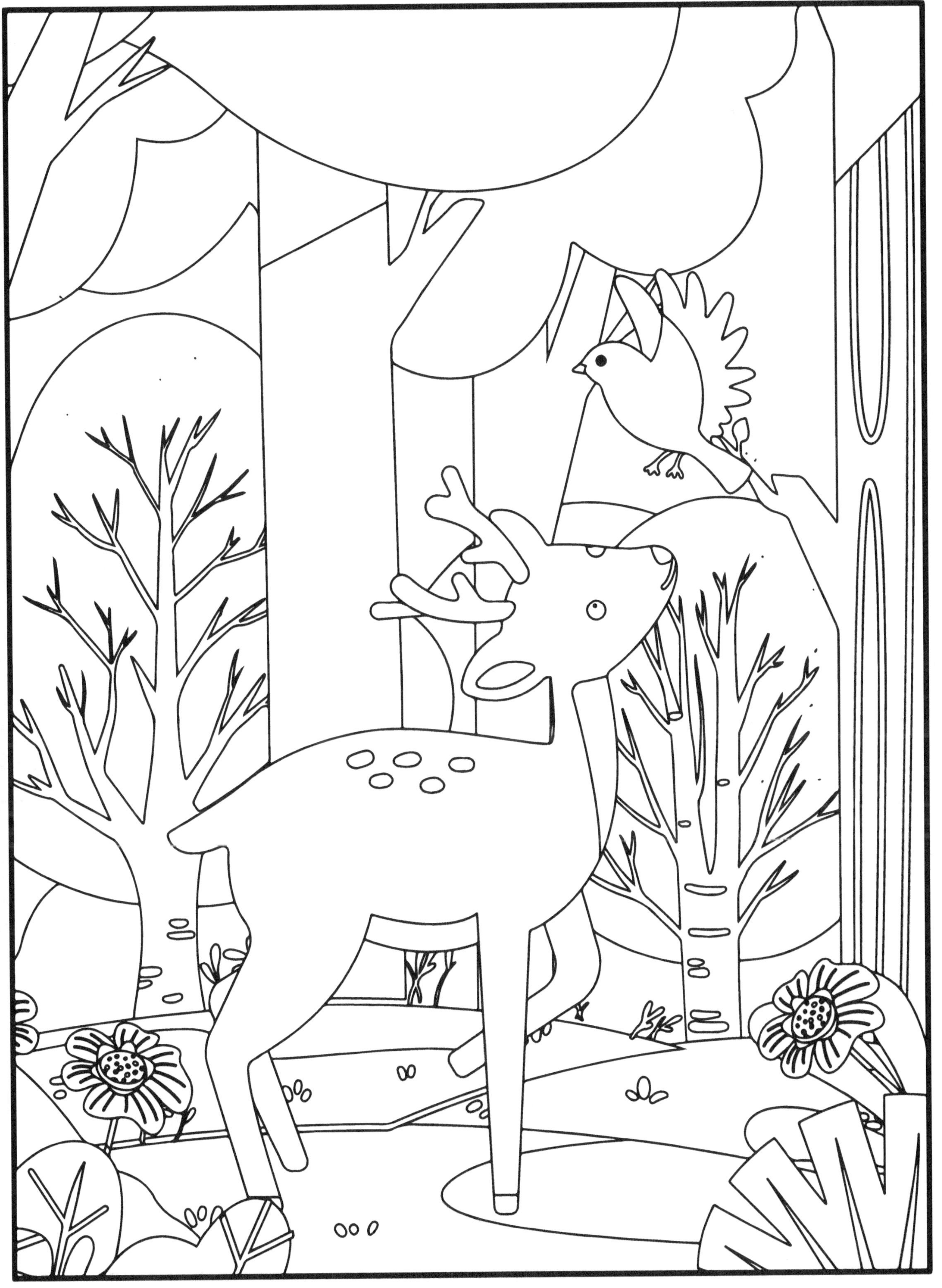

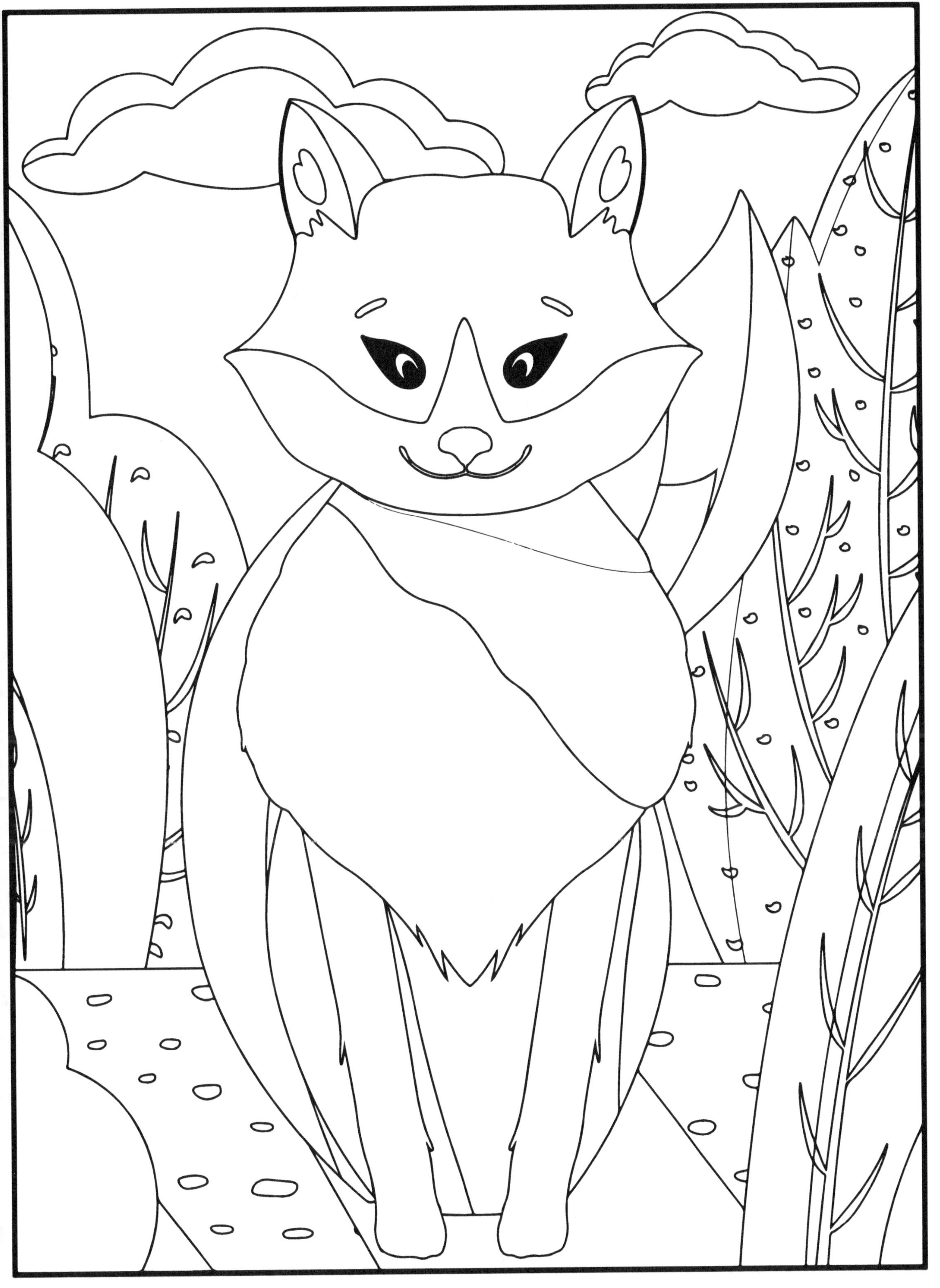

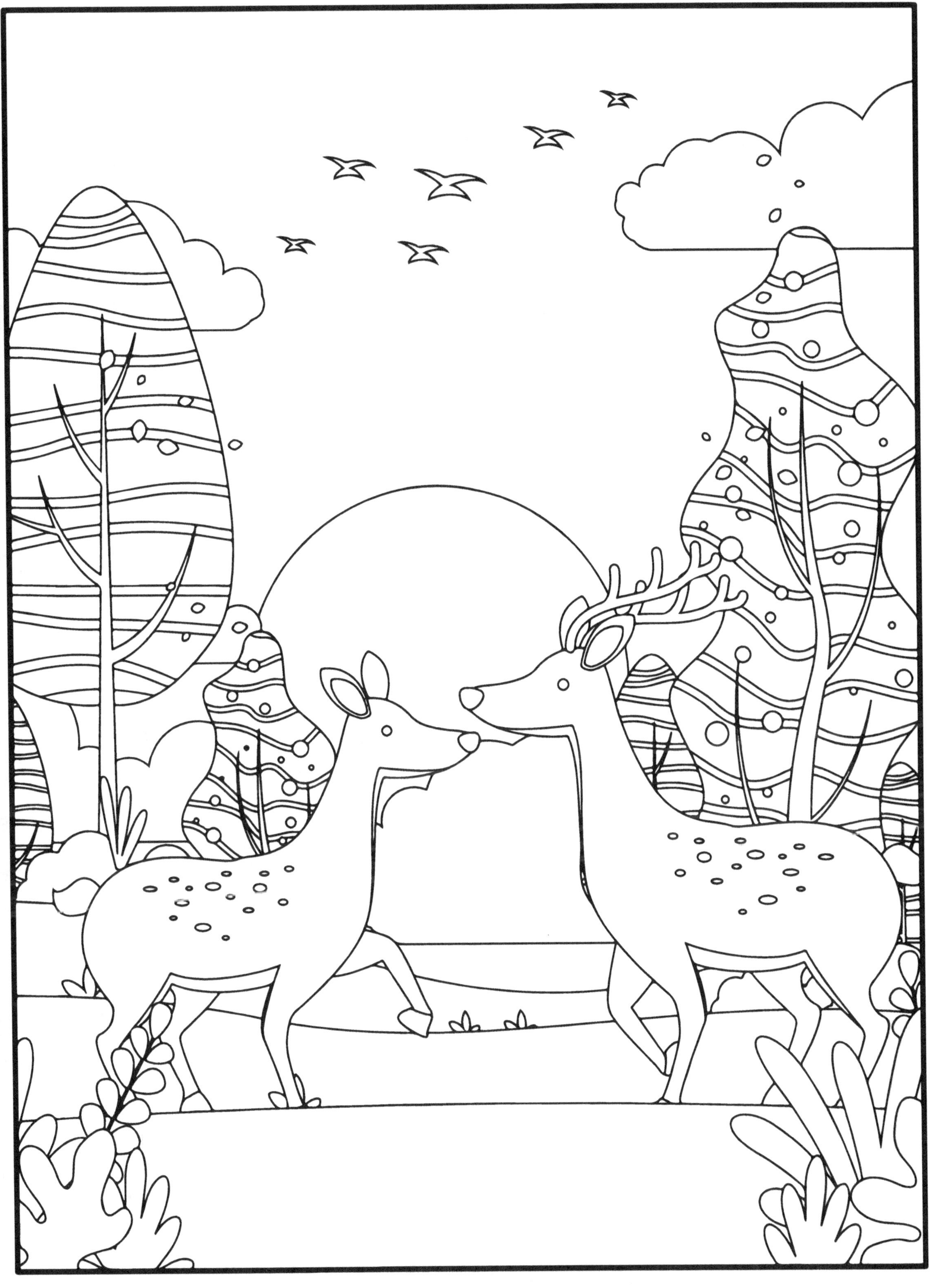

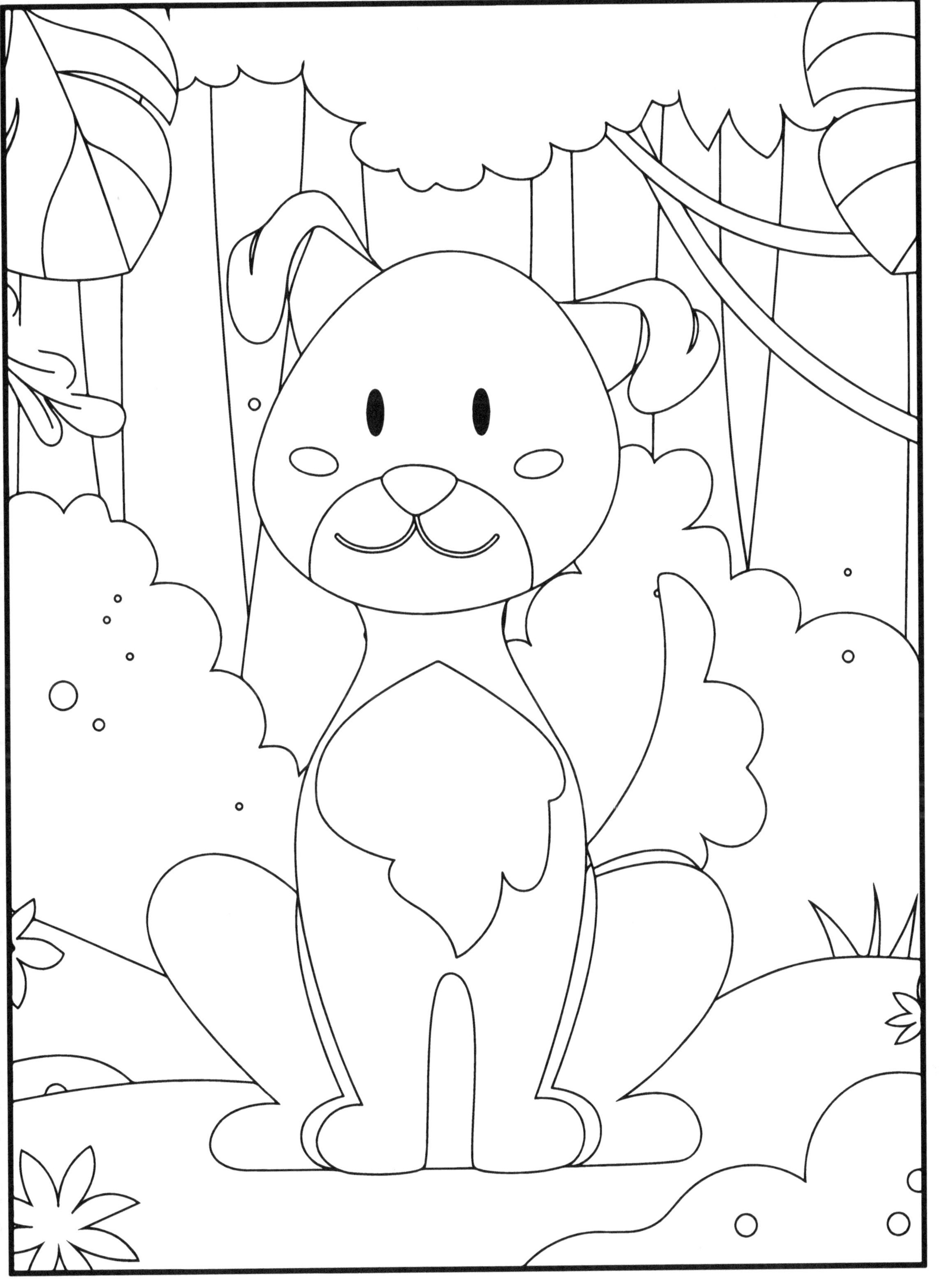

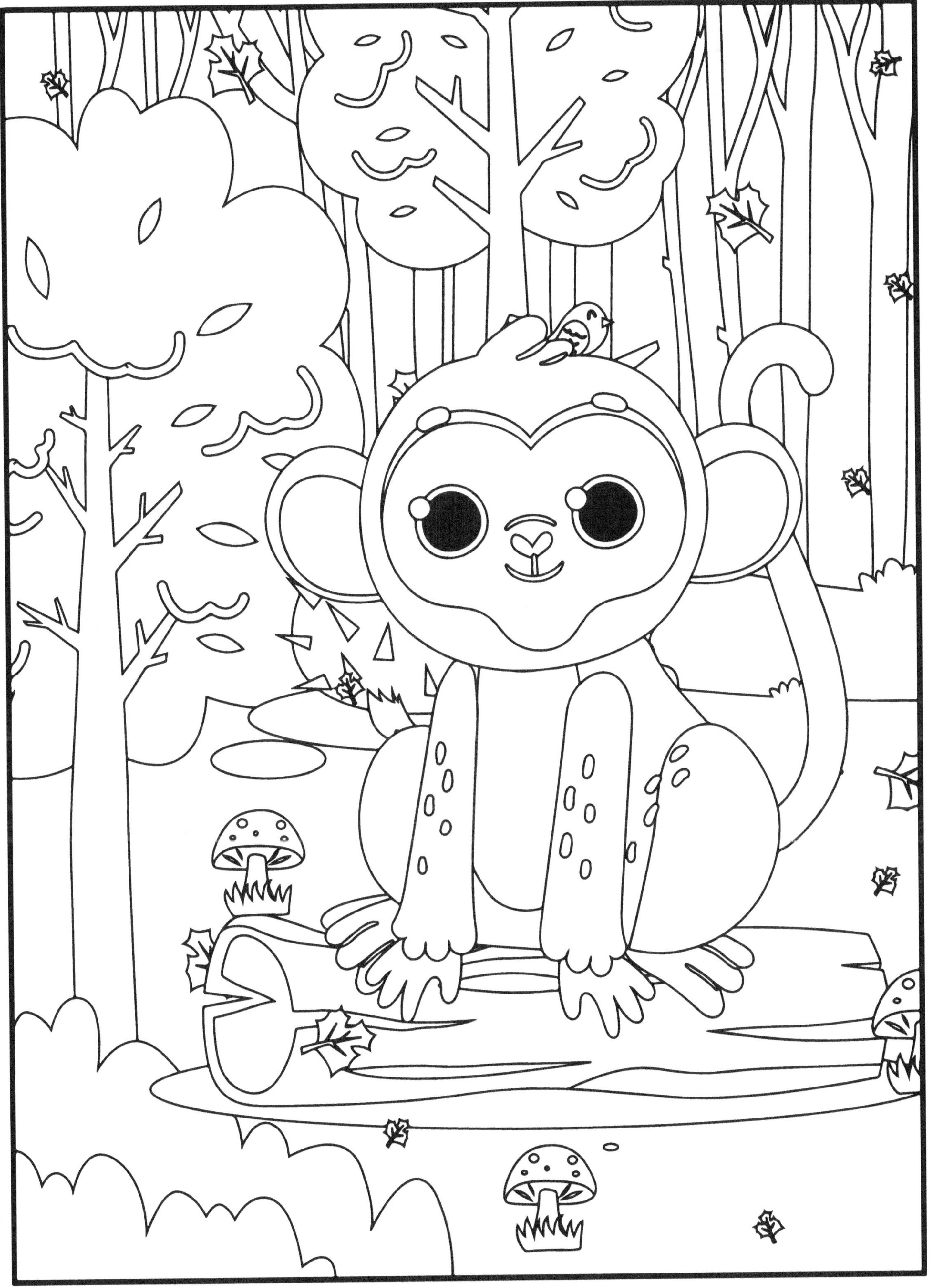

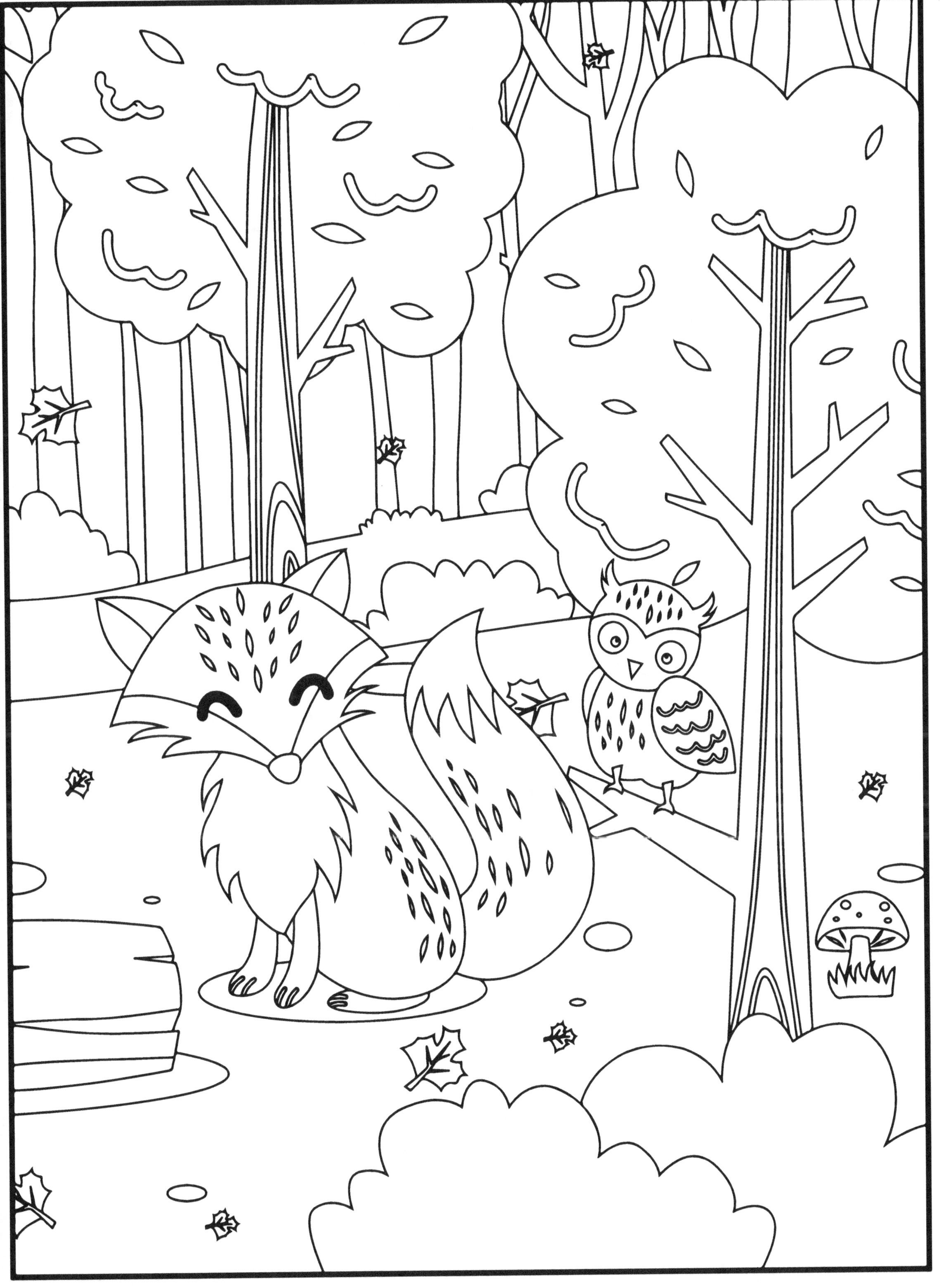

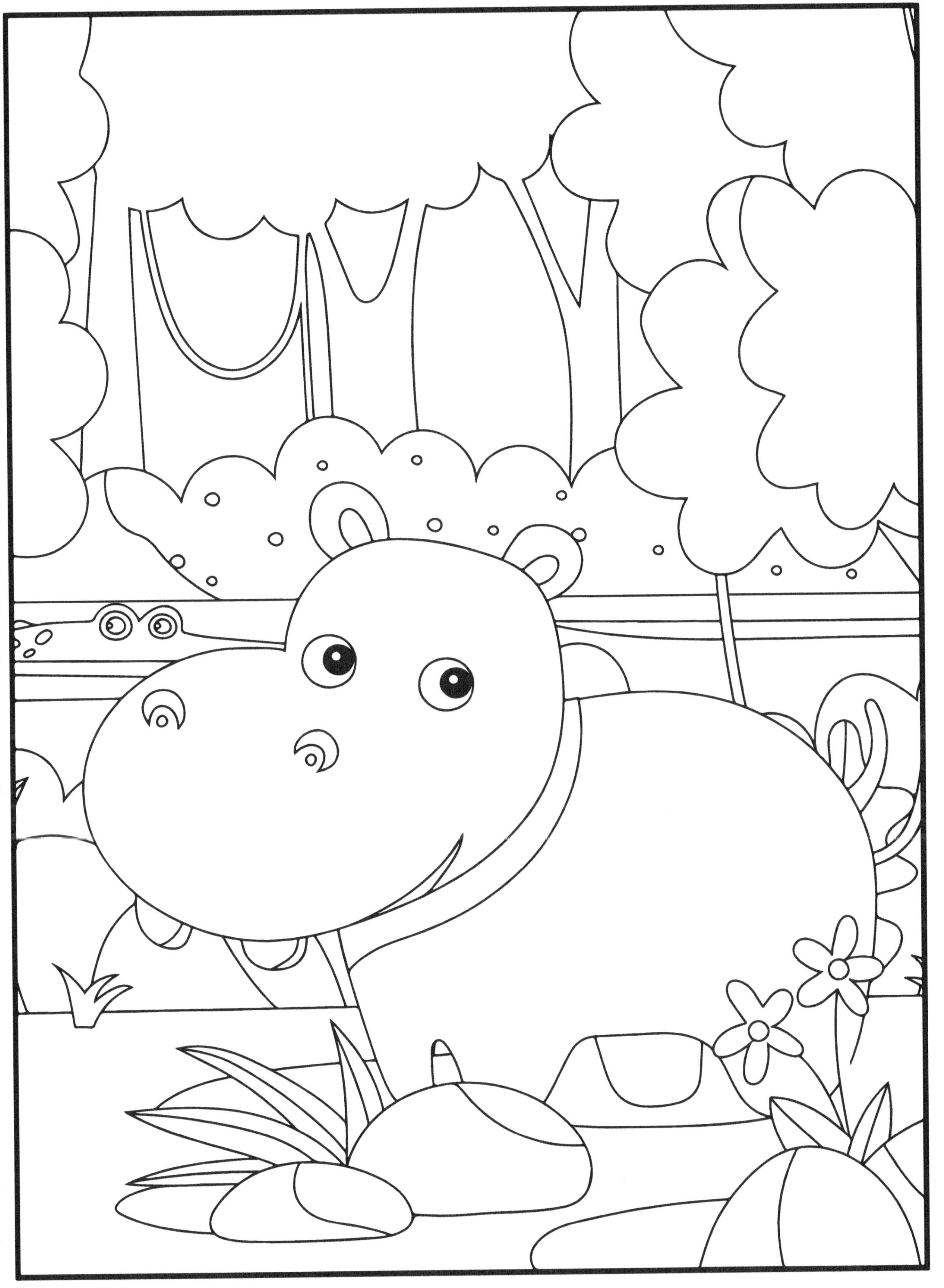

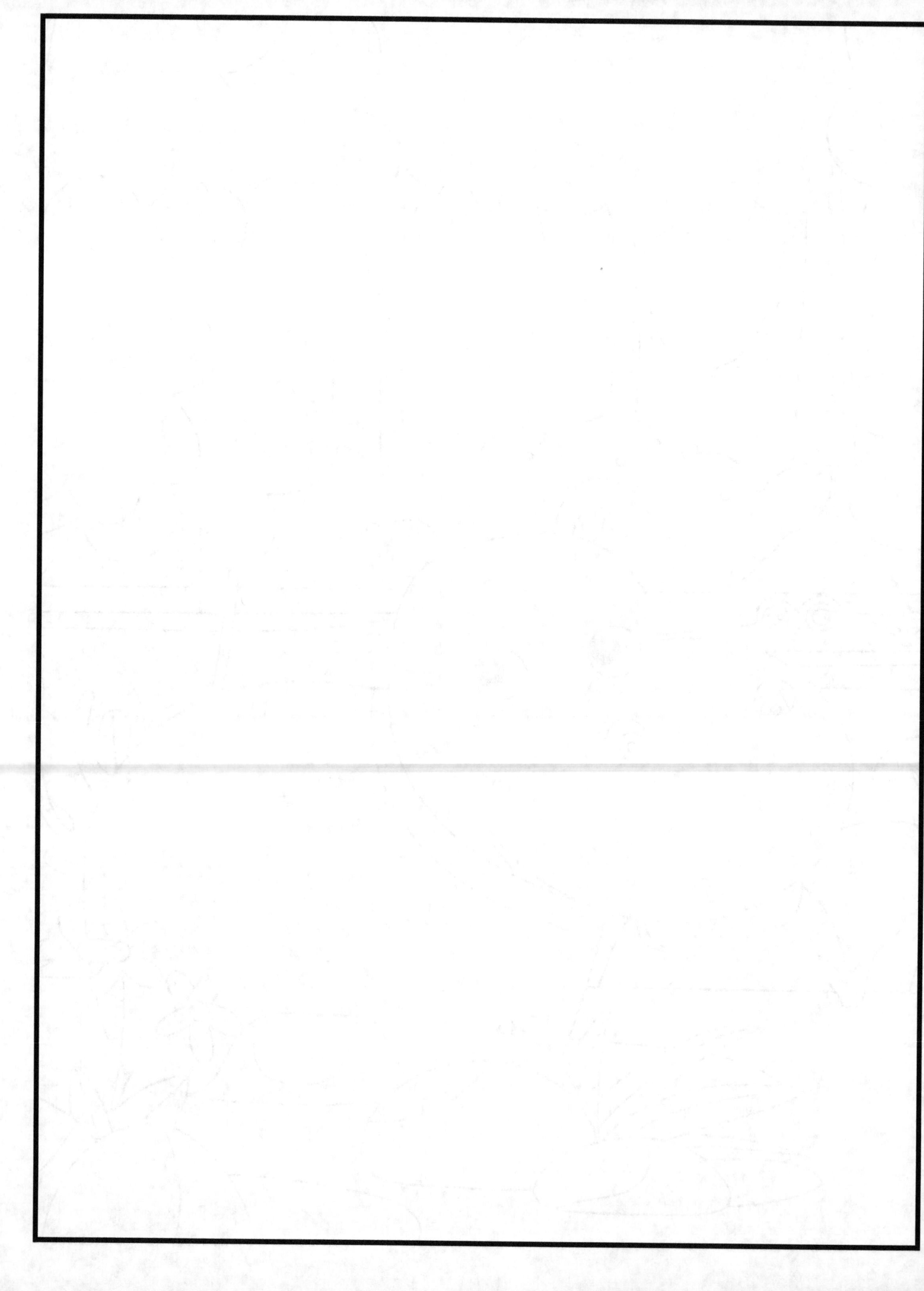

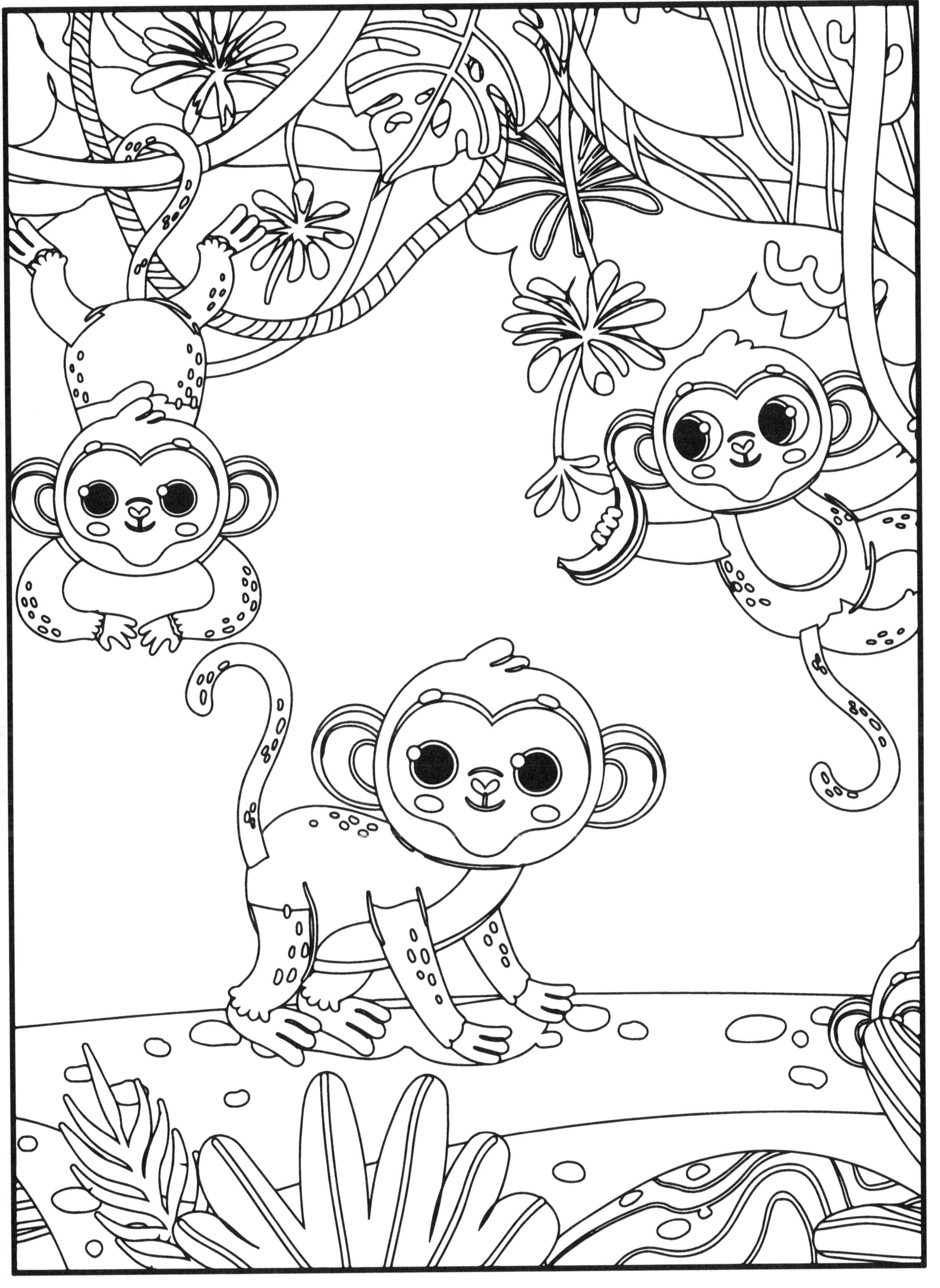

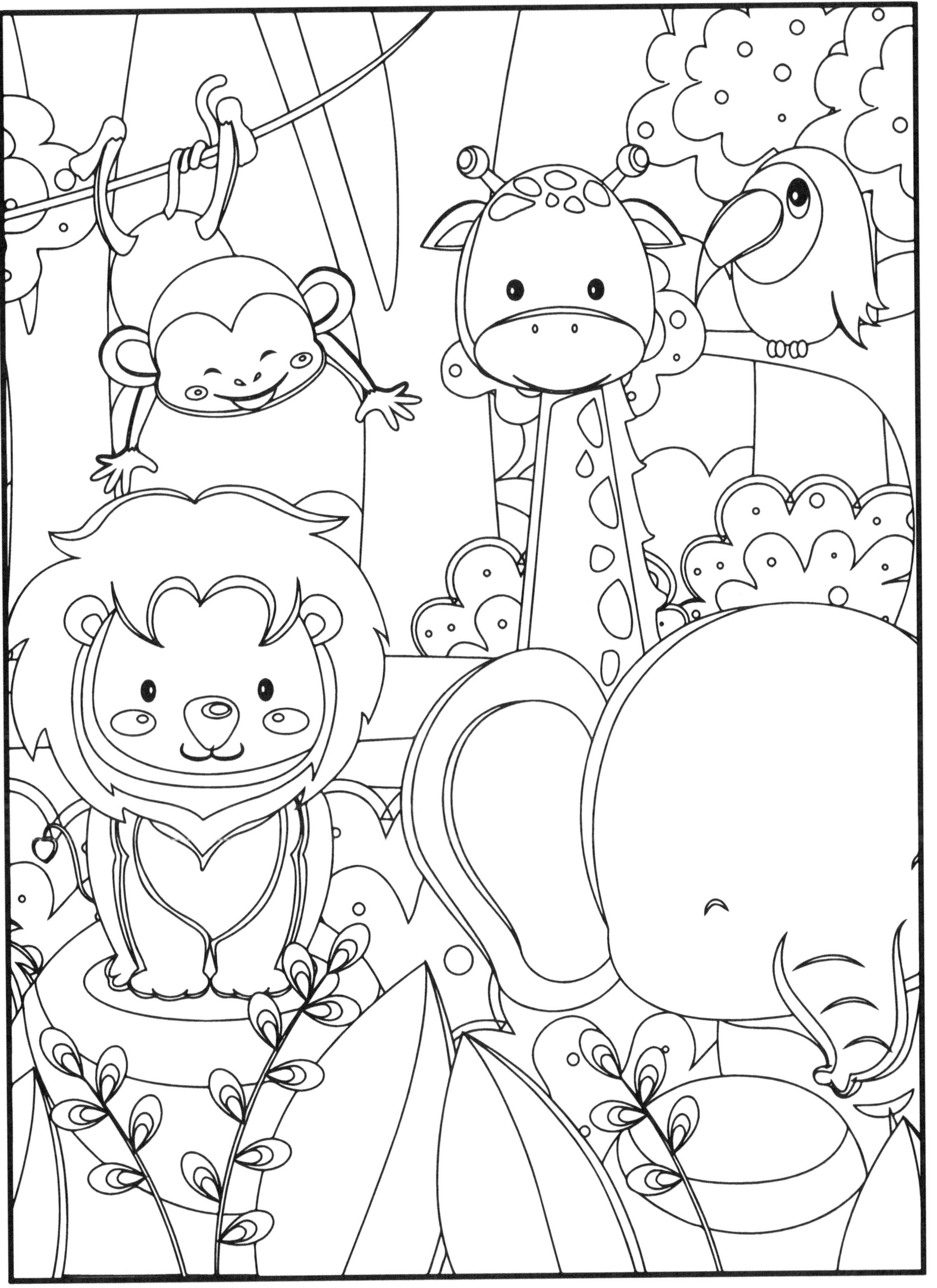

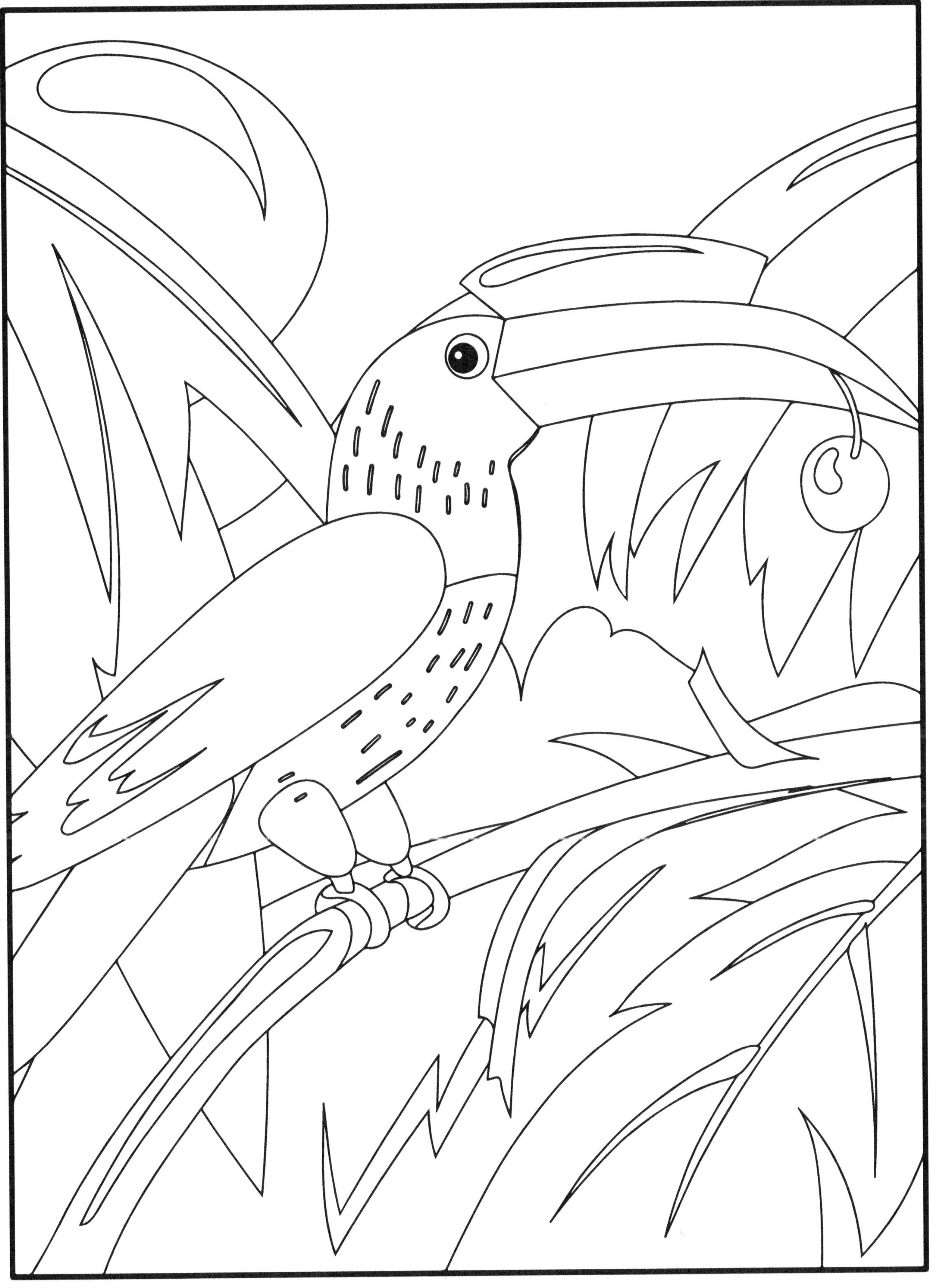

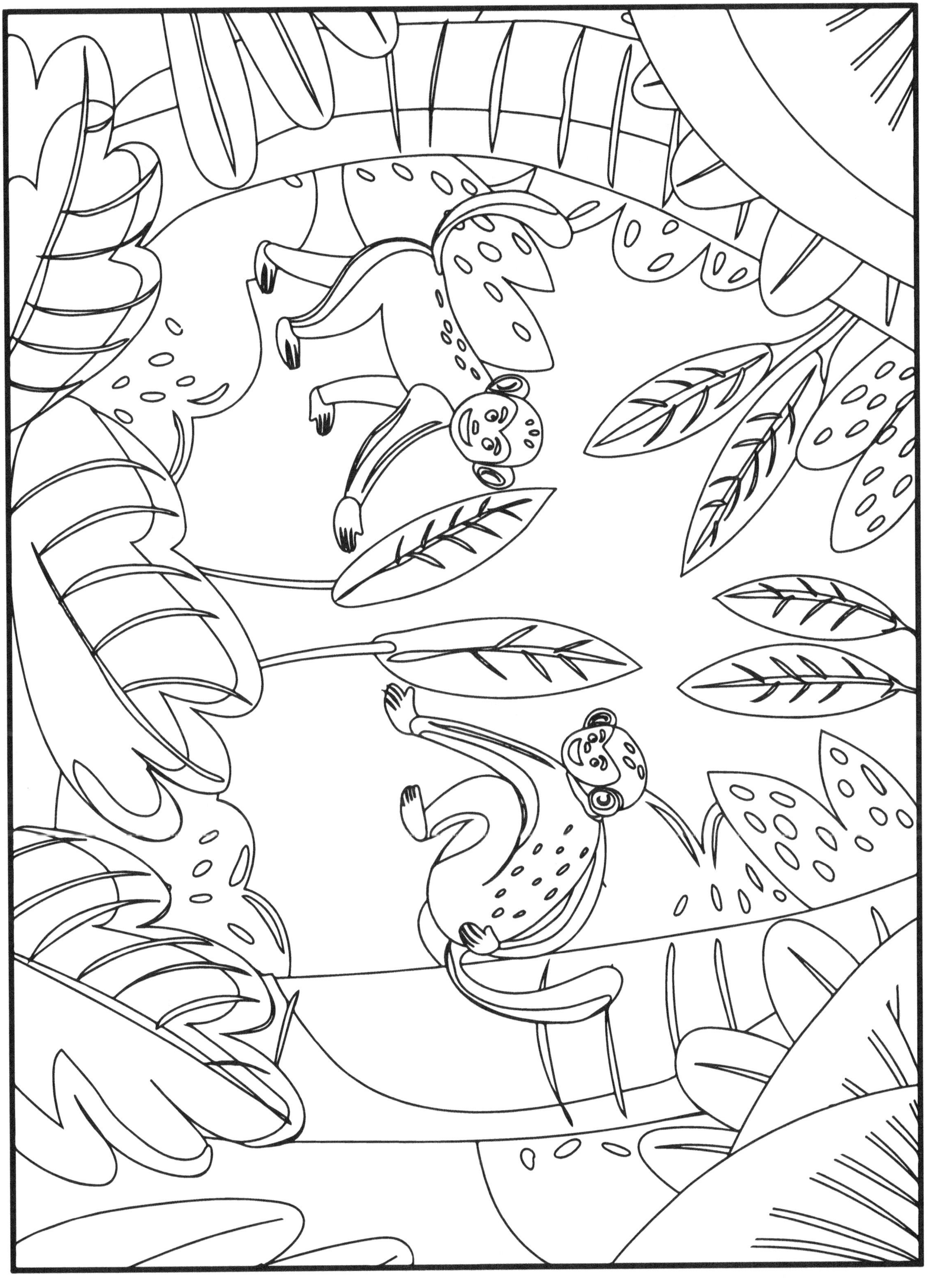

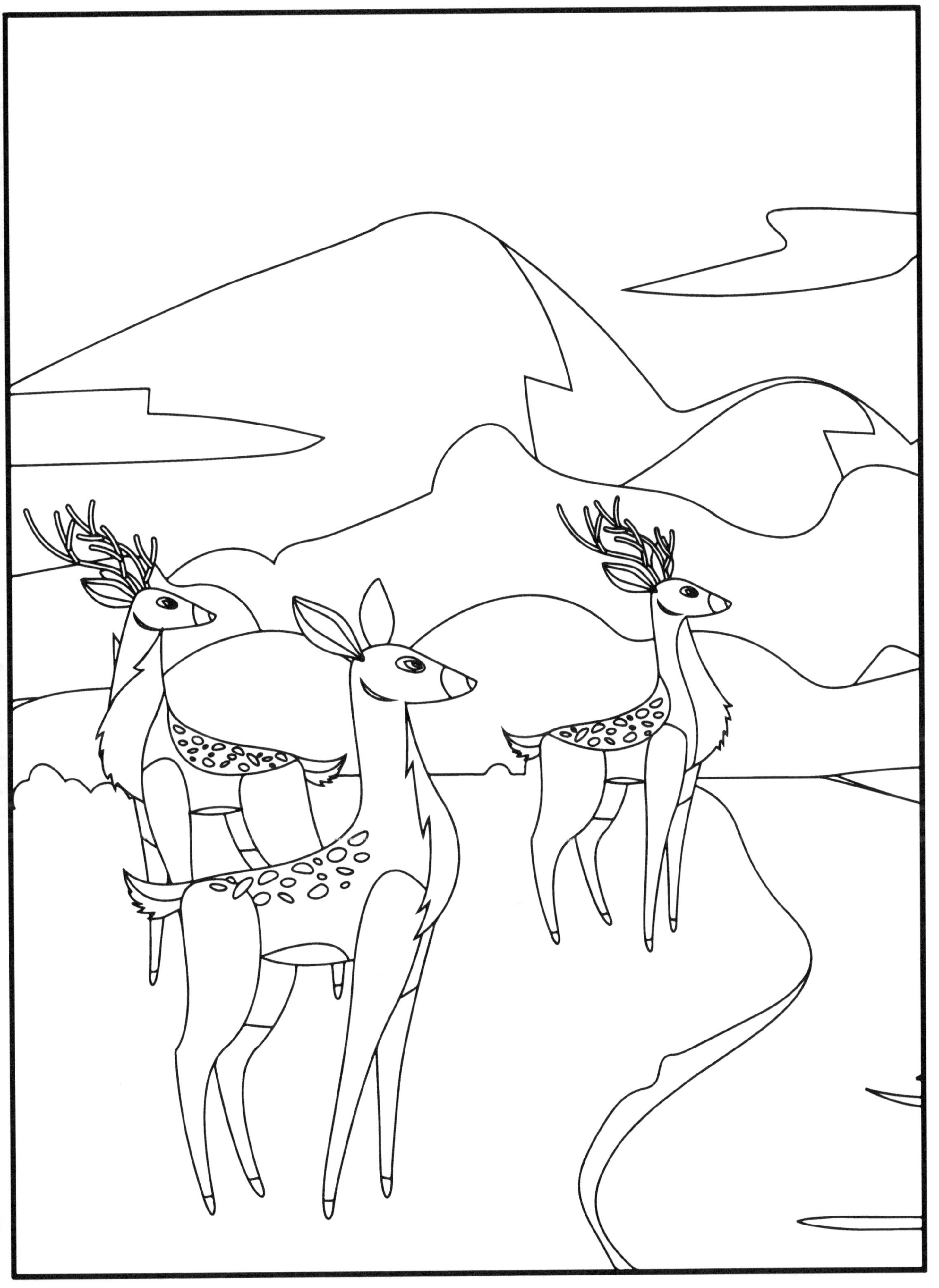

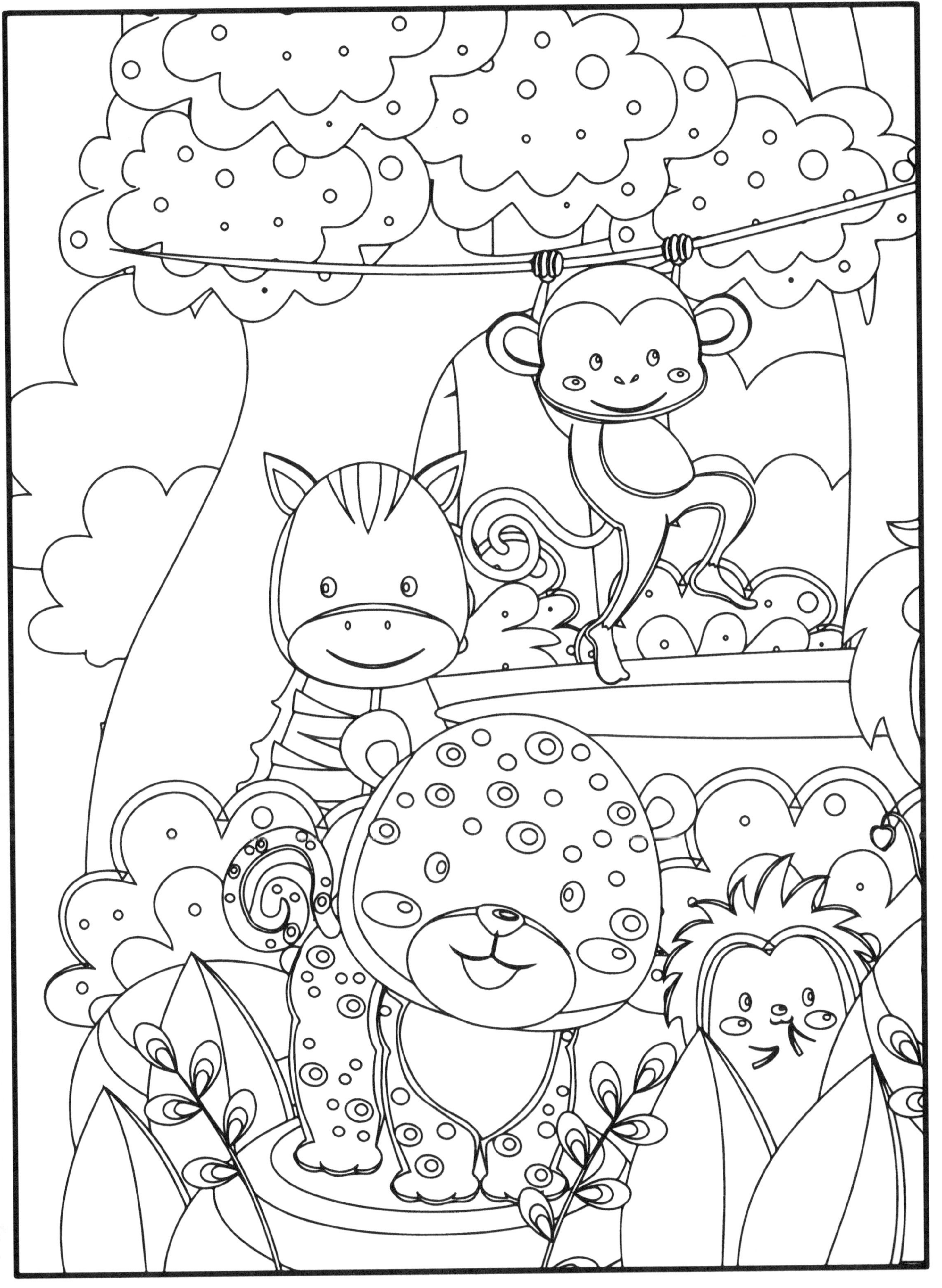

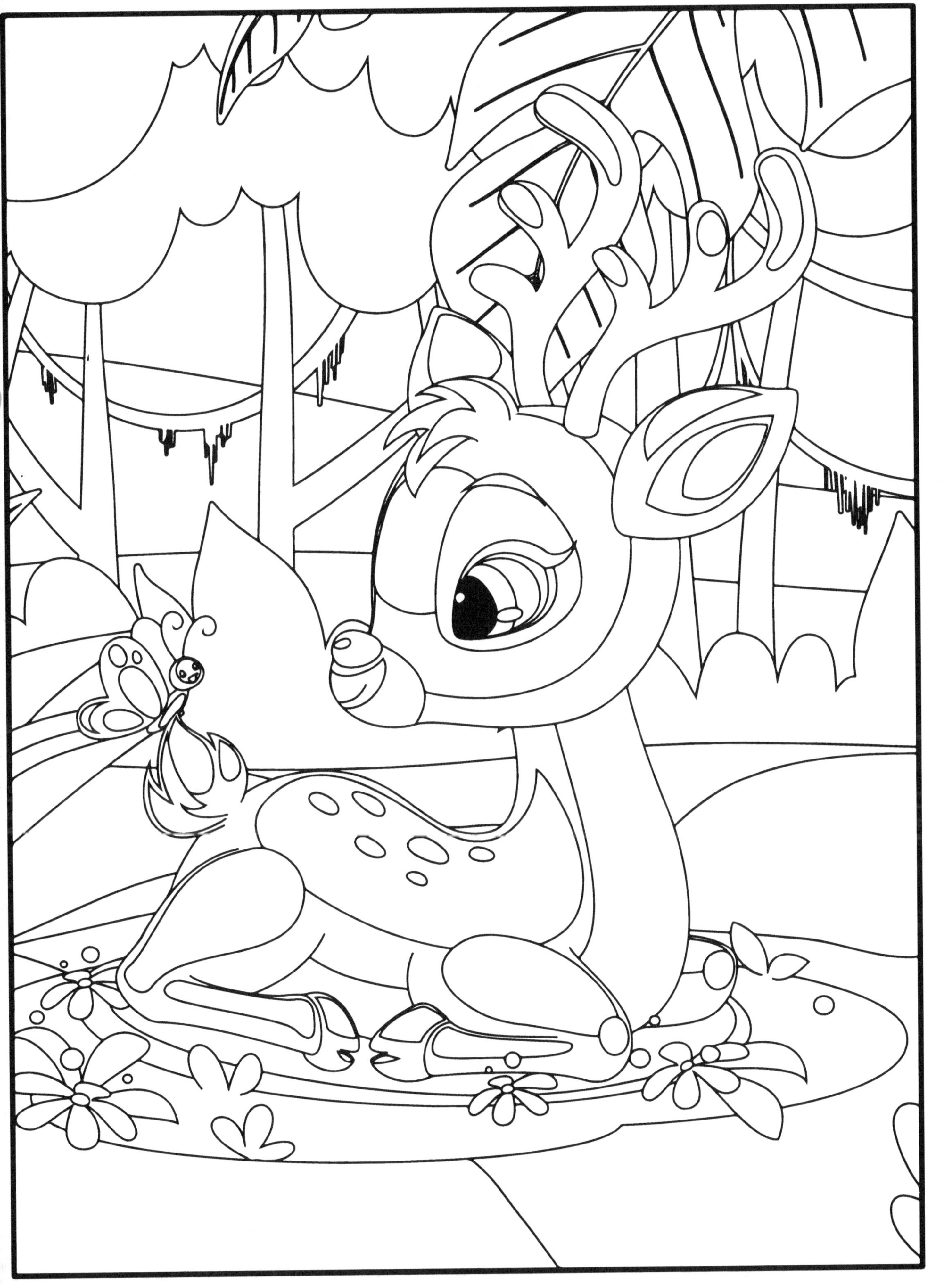

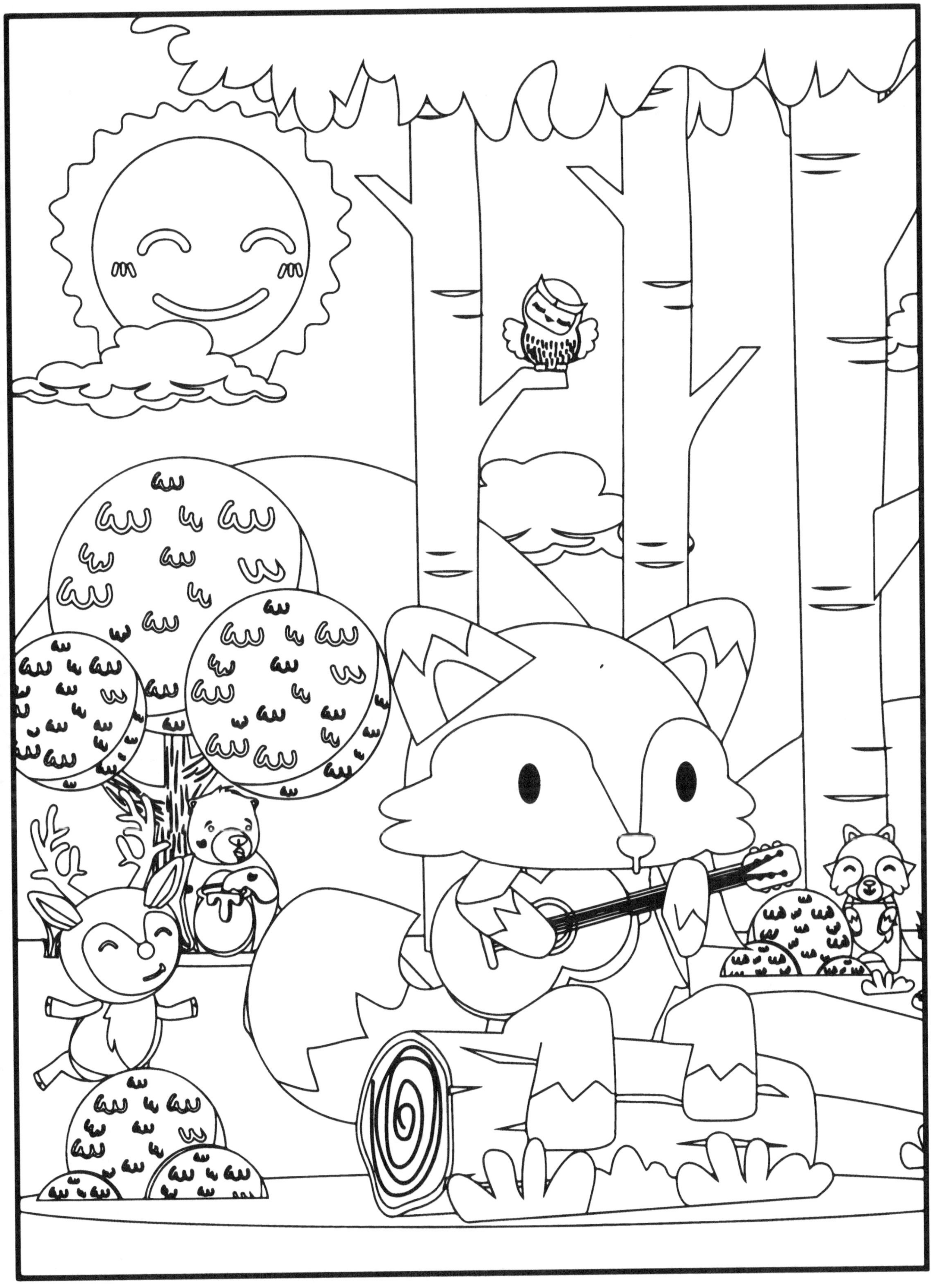

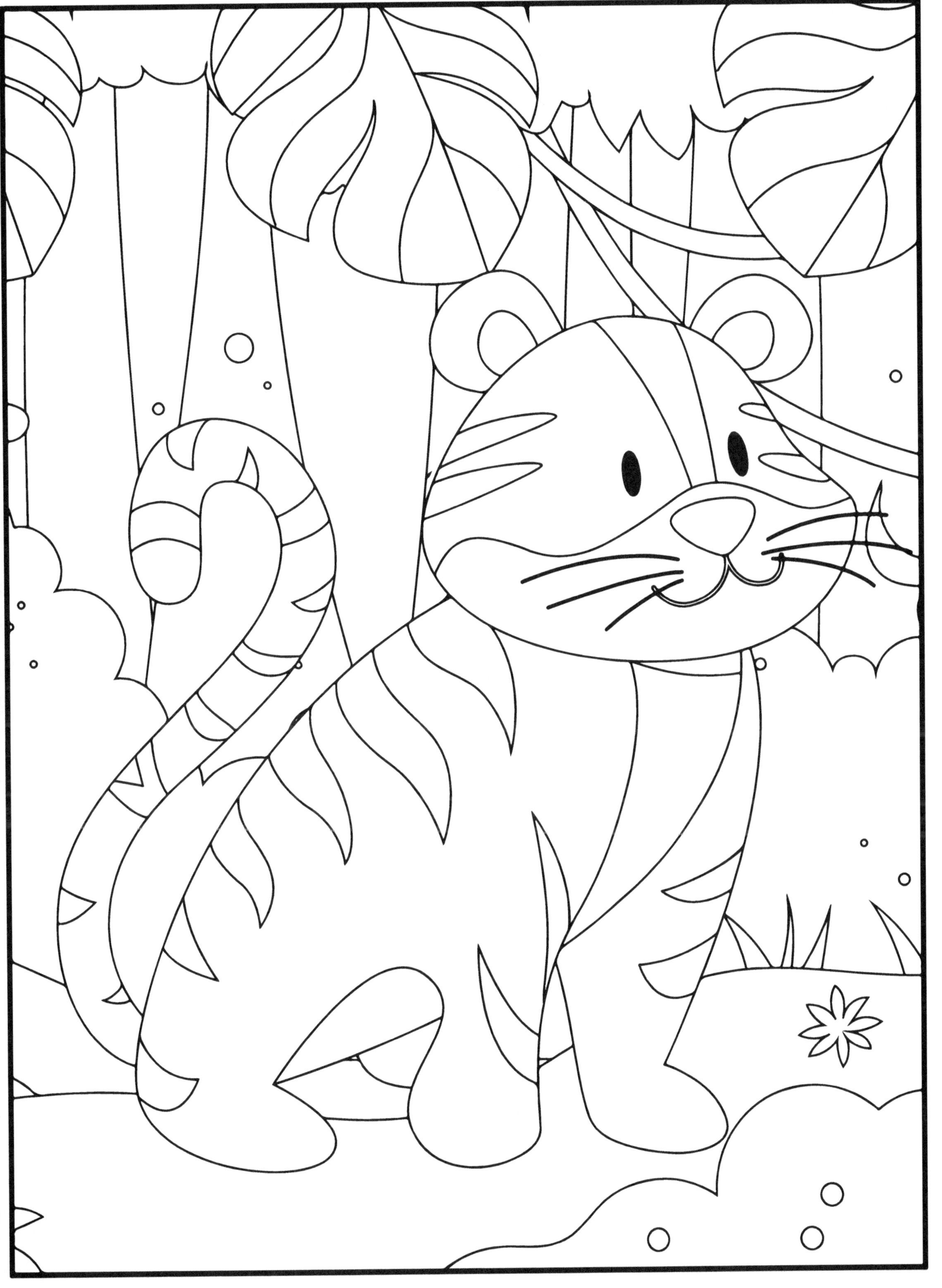

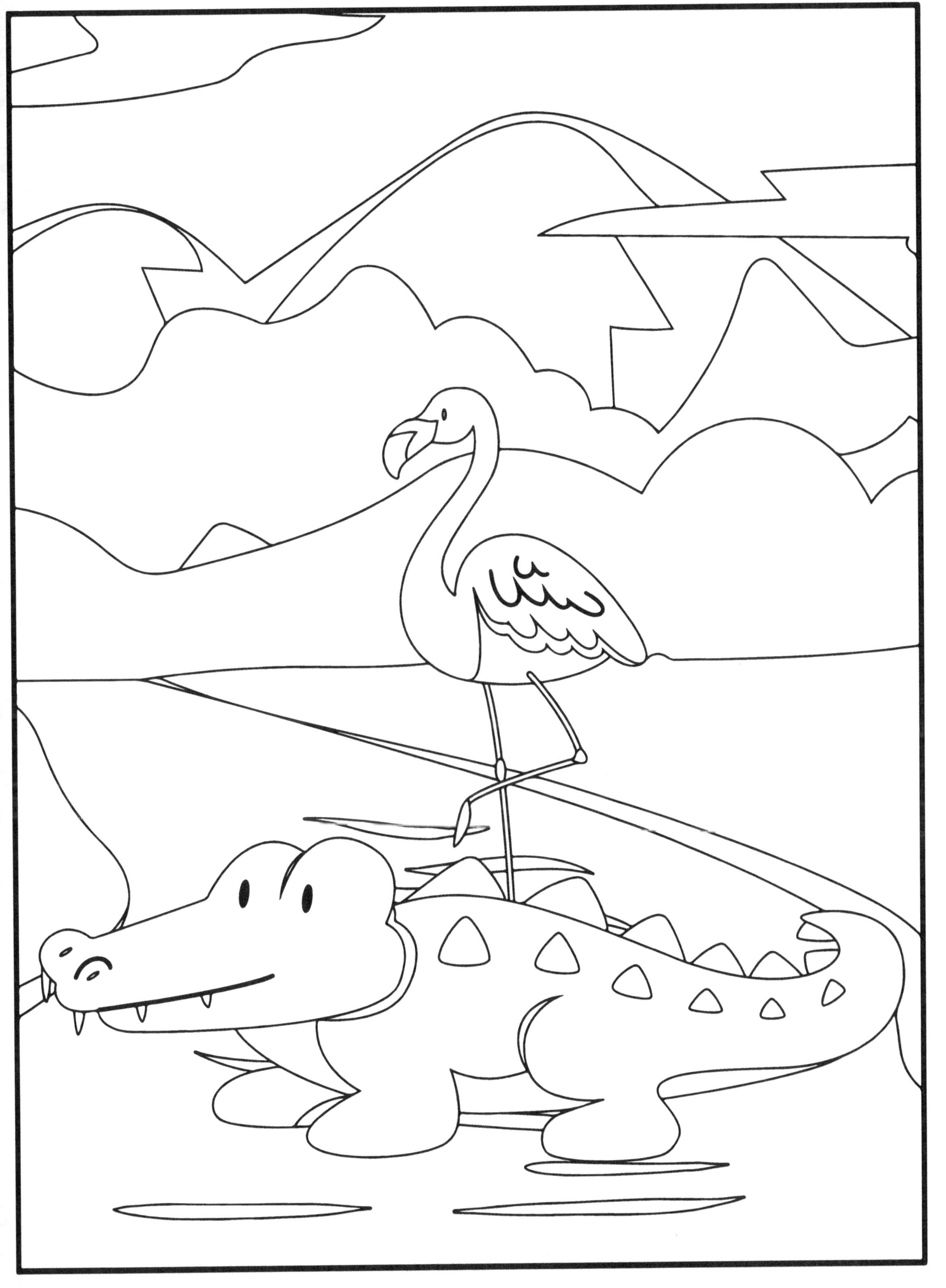

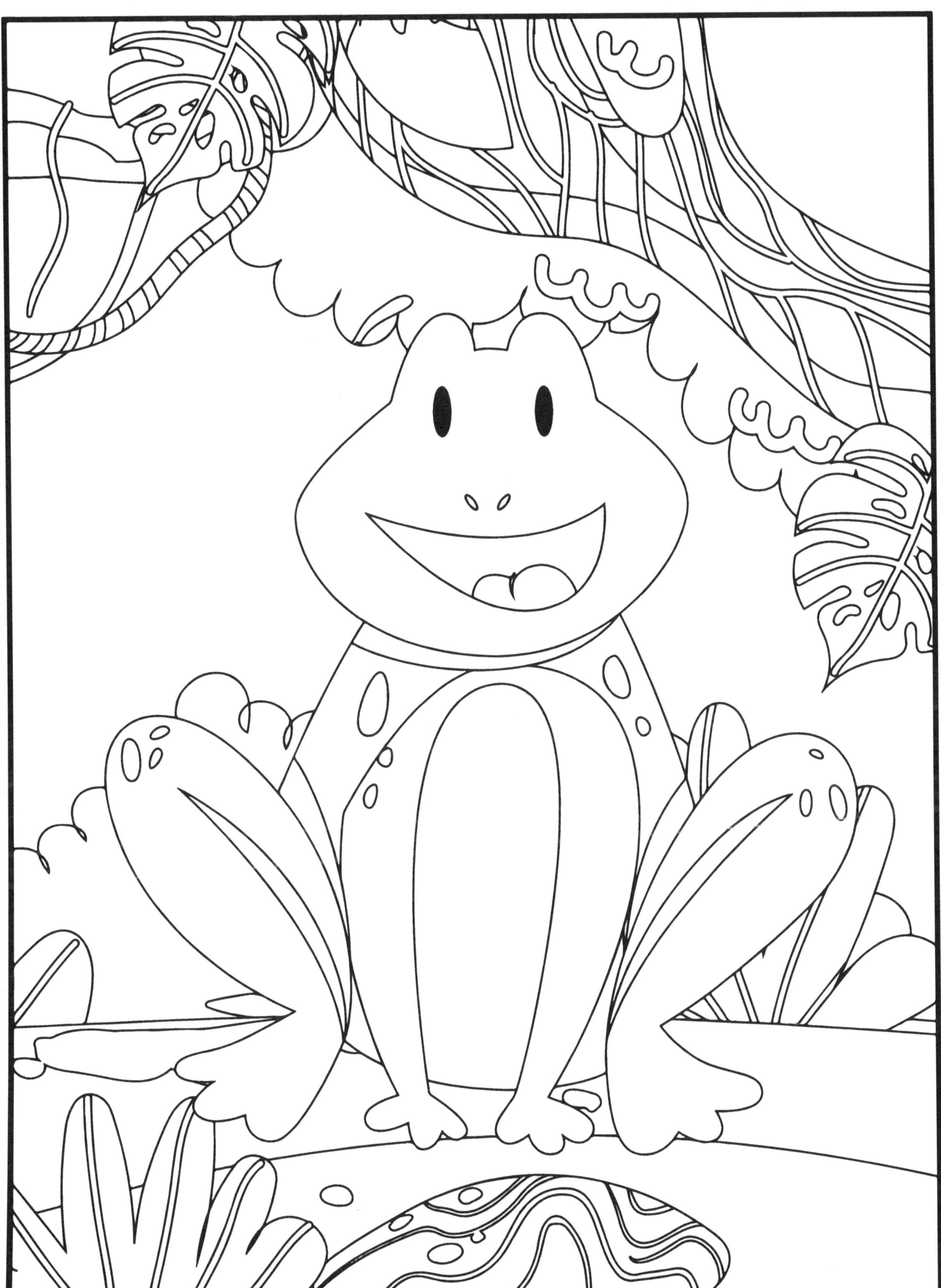